Wood Nymph Seeks Centaur

BY THE SAME AUTHOR

Fiction

Weetzie Bat
Witch Baby
Cherokee Bat and the Goat Guys
Missing Angel Juan
Ecstasia
The Hanged Man
Primavera
Baby Be-Bop
Girl Goddess #9: Nine Stories
Dangerous Angels: The Weetzie Bat Books
I Was a Teenage Fairy
Violet and Claire
Nymph: Nine Erotic Stories
The Rose and the Beast: Nine Fairy Tales
Echo
Wasteland
Beautiful Boys: Two Weetzie Bat Books
Goat Girls: Two Weetzie Bat Books
Necklace of Kisses
Ruby
Psyche in a Dress
Blood Roses
Quakeland
Pretty Dead

Poetry

How to (Un)Cage a Girl
Open Letter to Quiet Light

Nonfiction

Zine Scene: The Do-It-Yourself Guide to Zines
Guarding the Moon: A Mother's First Year

Wood Nymph Seeks Centaur

Seeks Centaur

A Mythological Dating Guide

Francesca Lia Block

with illustrations by Fumi Mini Nakamura

NEW YORK BERLIN LONDON

Published by Bloomsbury USA, New York

All papers used by Bloomsbury USA are natural, recyclable products made from wood grown in well-managed forests. The manufacturing processes conform to the environmental regulations of the country of origin.

LIBRARY OF CONGRESS CATALOGING-IN-PUBLICATION DATA

Block, Francesca Lia.
Wood nymph seeks centaur : a mythological dating guide /
Francesca Lia Block.—1st U.S. ed.
    p. cm.
ISBN-13: 978-1-59691-622-7 (hbk.)
ISBN-10: 1-59691-622-2 (hbk.)
1. Dating (Social customs) I. Title.

HQ801.B626 2009
306.73—dc22

2009008174

First U.S. Edition 2009

1 3 5 7 9 10 8 6 4 2

Designed by Maria Elias

Typeset by Westchester Book Group
Printed in the United States of America by Quebecor World Fairfield

For Lydia (Fairmaid) Wills and Reg E. (Gracefully Maturing Satyr) Cathey

Contents

Wood Nymph Seeks Centaur

Introduction

You are lost in a dark forest, surrounded by gnarled trees that block out the sun and moon. The paths twist and turn and seem to lead nowhere. Strange creatures that both attract and frighten you lurk in the shadows.

This is not just any wood—it is the dating forest. How do you survive? How do you find your way without a guide? The answer lies here.

My last boyfriend had curly hair that formed little horns on his head, a neat beard, well-developed haunches, and small, hooflike feet. He was lusty in bed and graceful on a skateboard. He took softly lit nude photos of me (mostly of my rear end, to be precise) and whenever I asked how he was when I saw him, he gruffly whispered in his thick accent, "Better now." Once he told me he had never felt as close to anyone as he did to me. But at the same time he didn't like to be tied down and he kept our relationship a secret for months. He still seemed quite attached to his young, beautiful ex-wife. When we broke up, he seduced his next girlfriend with the exact same tactics he had used on me. He took her photograph and even made her the requisite CD mix. I wondered whether he used the same songs. I watched him speaking softly to this new woman with his sexy accent, doing skateboard tricks to impress her, or standing quietly by while she leaped around in front of him, just as I had once done. I was devastated. What had I done wrong? How was I lacking? I couldn't figure out what had happened or how I had fit into the dynamics of the relationship. I felt that I didn't understand at all the man I'd spent a year with.

So I started dating, mostly on the Internet. Where else these days? It was the first time in my life I had really dated. I had been married for seven years, and before that had had only a few long-term relationships. All my past relationships had been chance encounters or introductions through friends, but these approaches felt too limited or random now. The Internet seemed to offer a world of possibilities.

But before I knew it, I had wandered into a dark thicket and lost my way. I was in a foreign, twisty, tangled forest without a map or a guidebook to help me understand all the new creatures that surrounded me. Which one was best suited for me? Who were they? For that matter, who was I, really? I was a loving single mother of two young children, a published writer, a loyal friend, a shoe fetishist, a part-time yogi, wild dancer, and love obsessive. And now I was also a dater. But what kind? And what kind of male dater should I be looking for as my potential mate?

At first I tried to answer these questions by jumping into emotional and sexual relationships with too many people, and much too soon. I knew I needed some guidance, but what kind?

When I was a little girl my father told me Greek myths as bedtime stories and my mother read fairy tales aloud. I loved to draw mythological creatures—fairies, mermaids, fauns chasing nymphs. As an adult I wrote about them in my novels and short stories. Myths and fairy tales are a part of me, a part of how I think about the world. Why had I cut myself off from them when it came to such an important aspect of my emotional life—dating? They had provided me with so much sustenance through the years (emotional and actual—writing about them is how I make my living). So why not draw on them now, when I really needed them?

I began to look at all my past relationships in this context. My ex-boyfriend was a Satyr. The ex before that was a Faun. I had had coffee with Giants. I had never become close to a Centaur. I had never even met a Woodsman, but for the first time I thought I might, because I was at last able to see and define him for what he was.

As for myself? I thought about it for awhile and determined that I was a Wood Nymph.

I recalled all my failed relationships, and when I looked at them through the lens of mythology, they no longer seemed so devastating. I felt seen, if only by myself. I felt a sense of order. Of course the Satyr left me. Of course I couldn't stay with a Faun. I was a Wood Nymph! It was like trying to date the wrong astrological sign. You might be able to triumph over fate in certain cases, but the odds are against you, so if you fail you needn't be discouraged. Just move on.

My restless writer's mind, which likes to make sense out of everything, felt instant relief from the mythological dating exercise. I did it more and more. I could go into a room and classify almost everyone immediately. My friends of all ages, genders, and mythological types joined me, categorizing themselves and their dates, challenging me ("So-and-so doesn't fit into any of your categories. You need a new one."), and adding their wonderful insights.

This mythological dating guide is the first and only mythological classification system to help all those experiencing the highs and lows of seeking a mate, or just a date. It's a way to discover more about yourself and others. It's a way of looking at others that is as old as the forests, lakes, and hills from which the initial types originated. After all, if the fairy tales are what we are looking for in our real lives, why aren't we turning to them for guidance? If you want a Tree Elf in your life, you must learn to recognize him. You may not even realize that you need a Tess and not a Pixie. This book will help you sort through the different types and will give you help in dealing with them. Once you see your Satyr, how do you avoid the heartbreak that he has a tendency to visit upon you? What is the best way for the Urban Elf couple to spend their time? What's a Centaur like in bed, and can he ever be happy with a Brownie, or is he more sexually compatible with a Fairy? It may be a forest out there, but with this guide, I promise you'll find that there are some friendly creatures around to support you and help you find your way. You just have to be able to spot them. And that may help them see you, too, which is what we're all really looking for.

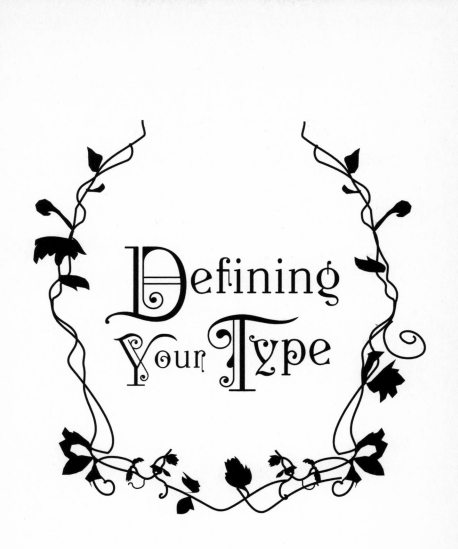

Defining Your Type

Before I tell you about the different types in detail, I am offering you a way to find out which one you truly are. You may think you are one type, based on name alone, but this section will provide you with the details that define the types on a deeper level. Find the paragraph that describes you best, without thinking about it too much. Then check the end (don't peek) to see which type you are. If you come out about even between two types, you are a combination. I'll explain this later. For now, read the descriptions with an open mind and remember to have fun. By defining your mythological type, you won't only have more insight into yourself and your relationships, you may be able to enjoy everything in your life just a little more. You might better understand why you like the people and things you do and begin to trust your true nature in pursuing more of what is meaningful to you.

It is possible for females to be one of the "male" types and vice versa, although some of the types, like Giants, Vampires, and Urban Elves, have closely related but distinct male and female versions. I have divided the descriptions into female and male types, but you may recognize yourself as either male or female despite your gender, so feel free to identify yourself using any of the summaries below.

Female Types

1. Do you wear low-rise jeans and not freak out too much if the crack in your rear accidentally shows once in a while? Have you either imagined working as a stripper or actually been one? Are you not very self-conscious about public displays of affection, or even public displays of animosity with your partner? Is sex important to you? What about creative expression— writing, painting, photography? Do you love to dance freely, without following steps or a routine, and will you do it almost anywhere? Do you like to listen to angry female singer-songwriters? Have you always passionately wanted kids? If you have them, do you love them with all your heart, even if they keep you constantly overwhelmed?

2. Are you compassionate by nature? If you are a mother, are you an excellent, if somewhat overprotective, caretaker? Do you work in the healing arts or just enjoy massage and yoga? Are you interested in alternative medicine and unconventional spiritual practices? Do you dress in flowing, loose-fitting clothing and rarely use much makeup? Do you listen to world music and read books about spirituality? Do you have a deep-seated reverence for nature and care tremendously about the state of the world? Do you sometimes have trouble with boundaries between yourself and the needs of others?

3. Are you smart and well read? Do you blog about, say, the new Charlie Kaufman film and make mix CDs featuring art-rock bands? Are you a devotee of musicians like Björk? Do you love to walk to cafés where you could spend hours drinking coffee, eating pastries, and working on your laptop? Would

you now wear or ever consider wearing a skirt with knee socks and cat glasses? Are you a closet romantic? Are you both a bit of a loner and a devoted friend?

4. Do you have more than twenty pairs of shoes? Do you spend hours on the phone counseling your girlfriends about their romantic troubles, but are you less likely to reveal your own? Can you get dressed in the perfect outfit at a moment's notice? Is shopping one of the things that helps cheer you up the most? Is food a very important sensual pleasure for you, especially dessert, but are you careful not to overeat? Do you love flowers and often give them to your friends? Do you like music that could be described as "pretty"? Do the words ethereal and/or effervescent describe you at times? Are you somewhat elusive?

5. Are the words fun and easygoing often used to describe you? Are you very social and always surrounded by friends who love you? Do you enjoy outdoor sports activities? In a relationship, are you looking for someone to go on adventures with? If you like someone, do you tell them directly and not bother with games? Do you enjoy fashion immensely but prefer looking cute and comfortable rather than overdressed? You may be this type.

6. Do you have good hair? You know you have good hair. You never really worry about not having good hair. Do you have a good singing voice? You can tell the difference between Prada and Dolce & Gabbana at a glance, can't you? You can spell Gabbana. Do males generally like you while other females might feel threatened by you? Do you sometimes insult others without meaning to do so? When you walk in the room does

everyone notice? If they don't notice, you make them notice at a moment's notice, right?

7. Are you relatively shy but with a passionate inner life? Do you deal with depression by getting in bed with a chick flick and a carton of ice cream? Are you maternal and gentle by nature? Do you listen to soothing singer-songwriters and read romantic literature? Is your house your pretty, cozy domain? Are your cupboards stocked with comfort foods that you like to cook up for a friend? Are you generally stable and down to earth, especially where your family is concerned?

8. When you're depressed do you yell about how angry you are or sing really loudly to your favorite song while driving on the freeway? Would you consider shaving your head? Are tattoos something you're very comfortable about getting? If you were a famous American poet, would you be Sylvia Plath? Are you looking for intensity above almost all else in a romantic relationship—that is, someone you can fight well with and then have great make-up sex with? Do others find you somewhat intimidating in spite of how sensitive you feel inside?

9. Is *savvy* a word that could describe you? Are you upwardly mobile in your career? Is your style classic and a little conservative? Are you practical but not immune to life's pleasures, like jazz music and a fine meal followed by chocolate? Your BlackBerry is never far from your fingertips, is it? Are you seeking a solid, loving, long-lasting relationship, and really won't settle for less?

10. Do you blend in fairly easily, but can turn the world on with your smile when you want to? Do you have a serious, dark

side that you sometimes disguise with laughter and teasing games? Are you someone who enjoys working out at the gym a lot to release the intense tension you sometimes feel? When you like someone, do you find it easier to become that person's friend than to involve yourself romantically? Is your personal style casual? Do you shy away from dressing in provocative ways most of the time? Have you ever been called a tomboy? If you answered "yes" to most of these questions, consider the fact that you may be this type.

11. Is edgy fashion one of your trademarks? Are you much more sensitive and shy than you appear? Do you enjoy an exciting nightlife and lay comparatively low during the day? Were you ever in an alternative music band? Do you have a lot of sexy black lingerie and spike heels? Do people sometimes think you are mysterious? Do you like to cultivate this impression? Do you love dark, romantic literature and music? If so, this may be you.

12. Are you known for your quixotic nature? Are you alternately charming or brooding and looking for a partner who will accept all the aspects of who you are? Do you have a definite edge that hides a more vulnerable side? On a date, do you enjoy sharing a drink at a dark bar? Will you run off your hangover (preferably in nature) the next day? Do you like music with an edge, maybe metal, and dress in a sexy but simple style? In spite of the fact that your relationships can be turbulent, are you always alluring enough to keep your partners intrigued?

If you identify most with the first description you are a
WOOD NYMPH.

If you identify most with the second description you are a
DRYAD.

If you identify most with the third description you are an
URBAN ELF.

If you identify most with the fourth description you are a
FAIRY.

If you identify most with the fifth description you are a
PIXIE.

If you identify most with the sixth description you are a
MERMAID.

If you identify most with the seventh description you are a
TESS (SHORT FOR GIANTESS).

If you identify most with the eighth description you are a
BANSHEE.

If you identify most with the ninth description you are a
HOBBY (FROM HOBGOBLIN).

If you identify most with the tenth description you are a
BROWNIE.

If you identify most with the eleventh description you are a
VAMP (FEMALE VAMPIRE).

If you identify most with the twelfth description you are a
WEREGIRL.

 Male Types

1. Are you an artist? Do you use your artwork to shut out the world when you are feeling down? Would your partners refer to you as the strong, silent type? Are they sometimes frustrated when you retreat into your creativity? Do you connect your sexuality with your creative urges? If you could pick a director to tell your life story on screen would it be someone like Julian Schnabel, Francis Ford Coppola, or Stanley Kubrick—men whose styles are wildly creative and at least a little dark?

2. Is spiritual connection one of the most important things in your life? Could your style be described as natural? Do you know about and seek out organic or generally healthy foods? Do you use the word *green* quite frequently? Do you enjoy hiking in nature, visiting natural hot springs, doing yoga, and giving and getting a massage? Are you familiar with the work of Walt Whitman? Perhaps you are this type.

3. Are you a smart, skilled techno guy with a creative side? Are you somewhat shy in social situations? Are you more comfortable communicating through technology than face-to-face? Is your style elegant with a slight edge? Do you wear stylish glasses? Are your filmmakers of choice people like Steven Soderbergh, Wes Anderson, and Spike Jonze—offbeat and intelligent? In a relationship, are you looking for a best friend to have really intense, fun sex with? Do you sometimes think that romance is overrated?

4. Do you pay a fairly large amount of attention to how you dress and what your home looks like? Is your personal style

trend-conscious with a bit of a rock-star edge at times? Are you quite social? When you like someone, do you pretend to be less interested than you are, even though you ultimately crave a passionate relationship? Can sex be like an art form to you—something you really enjoy and like to explore but is not always emotionally consuming? Is your work or are your hobbies somewhat creative?

5. Are you a family man who loves kids, animals, and kicking back outdoors? Do you value stability and passion about equally in a relationship? Is the phrase "good guy" sometimes used to describe you? Have you been told in a heated argument that you think too highly of yourself? Do you have the ability to cheer people up, just by your presence? Are you at least moderately successful in your career while considering yourself very successful in life? Would you consider your intelligence to be more emotional/intuitive than cerebral?

6. Are you a rugged, outdoorsy guy with a love of sports that take place in nature? Are you manly, laid back, and easygoing? Can you give off a protective vibe? Do you dress in casual clothes almost all the time? Is your work less important to you than your passion for surfing/biking/snowboarding (or perhaps you've converted that passion into your profession)? Is water in some form important to you? Do you celebrate an offbeat spirituality? What do you think—is this you?

7. Are you often described as gentle but have a temper, too, even if it's usually well contained? Is your presence solid and comforting, and are you very warm and humorous when you feel well cared for? Are you more sensitive than you at first appear? Are you looking for a relationship full of tenderness,

intellectual stimulation, and romance (probably in that order)? Do you like going to museums and collecting beautiful objects? Do you enjoy fine wine and dining and entertaining generously at your pleasant, comfortable home? Are you in general a very loyal partner?

8. Do you cultivate your image to attract sexual partners? Is *hot* a word you use often and is often used to describe you? Do you sport some kind of eye-catching body art, like piercings or tattoos? Are you talented at seduction? If you could write your life story, would it be similar to the work of Henry Miller? Do you like the sexy, edgy, action-packed films of Ridley Scott? Is there a brooding aspect to your personality? Have you had quite a large number of sexual partners? If you were to write a book would it be called something like *The Art of Seduction: An Intuitive Guide to Getting What You Want*?

9. Are you skilled at intelligent banter? Is *savvy* a word often used to describe you? Are you successful in your chosen field and enjoy living the good life with the money you make? Do you relate to the humor of Woody Allen? Would you call yourself a foodie? Are you opinionated? If, for instance, your date does not like chocolate will it bother you enough to question the relationship? Is your style rather classic, favoring simple clothing, jazz or classical music, and understated design choices? Are you this type?

10. Do you work out at the gym on a regular basis and have a lot of physical energy? Do you tend to look younger than your years, with a clean-cut, even boyish appearance? Are you seeking a fun, warm relationship, and are you less concerned

with all-consuming passion? Do you choose jobs that are less taxing so you can have time to enjoy your simple but pleasant life? Are you good with kids but don't come across as a strictly parental guy because of your youthful manner? This type may be you.

11. Do you define yourself a great deal by your darkly elegant and perhaps somewhat eccentric personal style? Do you admire the work of Tim Burton, David Lynch, Edgar Allan Poe, and others with dark artistic visions? Is music with an extreme edge to it a very important part of your life? Are you concerned with keeping up a certain appearance at all times? Are you a bit of loner? Do you feel more comfortable at night than in the day? Do you like to cultivate an aura of mystery?

12. Are you style conscious in a cool, subtle way? Would you wear a fedora with a short-sleeved button-down shirt to the right event? Are you known to have sudden mood swings? Are you soft-spoken but do you loosen up a lot after a few drinks? Do you like to experiment with exotic foods and unusual music? Are you up on politics and the arts? Is your day (or night) job less important to you than some private hobby you enjoy? In a relationship, are you looking for someone who will accept you as you are above almost anything else?

If you identify most with the first description you are a
CENTAUR.

If you identify most with the second description you are a
TREE ELF.

If you identify most with the third description you are an
URBAN ELF.

If you identify most with the fourth description you are a
GARDEN ELF.

If you identify most with the fifth description you are a
WOODSMAN.

If you identify most with the sixth description you are a
MERMAN.

If you identify most with the seventh description you are a
GIANT.

If you identify most with the eighth description you are a
SATYR.

If you identify most with the ninth description you are a
HOB (SHORT FOR HOBGOBLIN).

If you identify most with the tenth description you are a
FAUN.

If you identify most with the eleventh description you are a
VAMPIRE.

If you identify most with the twelfth description you are a
WEREWOLF.

If you have read all this and still don't see yourself, you are most likely a combination type. Certain types tend to combine more commonly than others, enough so that I have developed special names for these combos. For instance, I know many Mermaid/Fairies, called Fairmaids, and Wood Nymph/Fairies, called Fairnymphs. These combination types will be discussed following the description of the single types.

Now that you know what type you are, you can proceed to read more about yourself and others.

The
Types

Male Types

CENTAUR: THE ARTIST

Centaurs are a rare combination of intellect and physical prowess, although they can get lazy with their bodies and are not particularly self-conscious regarding their appearance. They often sport small, neat beards and casual, masculine attire as opposed to business suits. Some wear their hair long, and if they are vain about anything, it might be the condition of their locks.

Contradiction defines them. They are avid readers and quite scholarly but not immune to sensual pleasures. In general, the Centaur is soft-spoken but forceful. He may charm you with his gentle manners, but when he wants something he can become moody and even belligerent until he gets it. Centaurs can be serious and funny. They have subtle, sly senses of humor that can catch you off guard. They can be quite passionate in a romantic sense, although this same intensity can sometimes make them lacking in tact and even lead to aggression. A Centaur may also make a mess of your house by wearing his muddy boots indoors, leaving his dirty dishes in the sink, and pulling the sheets off your bed with his enthusiastic lovemaking.

This somewhat destructive aspect of the Centaur can be seen in his habitat. He is not the neatest of forest folk, and his abode is often strewn with piles of unwashed laundry, stacks of bills and papers, and whatever materials he needs to create with. There are usually some signs of his creativity, whether it be the paintings on the walls, the sculptures he has made, the screenplays he has written, or music he's recorded. When he gets absorbed in a project he loses all sense of time. He can lock himself in with his work for days and nights and hardly realize that he hasn't slept or eaten. Some less artistically inclined Centaurs can be found working in service positions, like teaching, or somewhere outdoors. They, too, can get carried away with work.

When he comes out of these sessions, a Centaur may spend a few days drinking and eating too much. He especially likes charming, inexpensive hole-in-the-wall restaurants that serve somewhat exotic international food. Another way the Centaur may get carried away is by overindulging in casual sex.

Although not as promiscuous as Satyrs or as emotionally detached as Elves, Centaurs do tend to separate their physicality from their intellect, so it is difficult to sustain long-term, integrated relationships with them. A Centaur does not take his sexuality lightly, however, and although he is able to separate the physical from the emotional, it may leave him feeling rather empty and melancholy. This in turn leads him back to bury himself in his work.

It is sometimes hard for Centaurs to find a balance between work and play. However, they are at their best when they can make space in their lives for regular meals, enough sleep, and strenuous exercise, while continuing to express themselves through their work. Unlike the Urban Elf and Tree Elf, who do this naturally and on their own, a Centaur may need a partner to help him find this balance. If they can take the passionate focus off their work for a long enough time, Centaurs, especially maturing ones, may be able to find loving relationships. However, their partners tend to feel a bit challenged. Centaurs may not run off with the next Nymph who comes along, but they won't commit as fully to you as they do to their creative or intellectual pursuits.

The psychological key to the Centaur is that he has learned to handle stress or anxiety by applying himself to his work, especially creative work. It is where he feels the most safe, alive, and at peace. Wood Nymphs and Banshees in particular understand this, as they are quite similar in the way they manage upset in their lives. If a Centaur's partner can be patient with his need to be alone and at work, she can enjoy a relationship with a deep, fascinating, and passionate creature.

When a Centaur is in the mood to leave his project, he will be a very attentive date. He will usually plan the evening, pick you up, graciously pay for dinner at a nice, if rather inexpensive place, and enjoy a warm, communicative sexual encounter with you. He will ask you how you feel about things but may not listen carefully to your answers. He will share things about himself, although not nearly as much as a Tree Elf or Giant will. Finally, he may find a way to include you in his creative process by writing a song for you, exchanging poetry back and forth via e-mail, collaborating on a screenplay, or painting your portrait. If you can charm a Centaur into including you in his work in this way, you can get closer to him than through any other method and find a way to tame his somewhat erratic moods.

I met a beautiful Centaur who captivated me. He was younger than I, with long, thick black hair; big, dark eyes; and large, sensual features. His body was tall and strong, though slightly out of shape from so many hours spent in the recording studio rather than running in the hills. What drew me to him more than anything were his creative gifts. He could pick up any instrument and play it. He could compose songs and sing them beautifully. I told him how wonderful I thought his commitment to his music was. He replied, "Not if you want to be in an intimate relationship with me, it's not." In spite of this warning I allowed myself to get close to him. The chemistry was electric and there was a sweet tenderness between us. I also felt I could handle his love affair with his music, as I have a similar relationship to my writing. But a young Centaur and a maturing Nymph may have trouble finding a way to be in a relationship, in spite of their matched creativity and powerful attraction to each other.

I will always have a special place in my heart for Centaurs, whether I end up with one or not. This is because my father was a Centaur, and Wood Nymphs usually have intense relationships with their dads. He was a fiercely creative painter who was not particularly interested in settling down to start a family until my mother captured him. He taught me how to express myself creatively without fear, guilt, or inhibition. Although he was quite loving, he could be withdrawn, especially when angered. This is also a Centaur trait and it had an adverse effect on this Nymph. He died before I had gained the maturity to be able to confront him with my issues, but if we had been able to have that discussion, he would have listened to me and helped me reach a resolution. Mature Centaurs are quite capable of going quite deep into relational issues if they are just slightly pressed. Remember this when you are dealing with one. Just don't be overbearing—they can become defensive and shut you out.

TREE ELF:
THE NATURE CREATURE

Tree Elves are much more comfortable in woodland areas than in cities and spend their spare time hiking, doing yoga, creating art projects, and enjoying healthy foods. They also love music, and when it is combined with an outdoor setting, like a festival in the desert or countryside, the Tree Elf couldn't be happier. They know a lot about diet, nutrition, and exercise and have been known to give unwanted suggestions about these things to their friends and lovers. Although this may be off-putting to some, most Trees are quite charming in the way they communicate. They are very social and have a lot of friends of all different types. A typical

Tree Elf adapts well to a variety of situations and is generally well liked. When he is feeling happy and secure, usually after creative expression, sexual attention from a variety of creatures, or relaxing activities like massage or yoga, a Tree Elf is particularly magnanimous, generous, and fun to be around. He usually inhabits a natural-looking, attractive environment with a lot of wood, organic materials, and plants. He may even have studied feng shui—everything is placed carefully where it belongs. He surrounds himself with pets and friends.

Unlike Urban Elves, who prefer metrosexual chic, Tree Elves like loose, comfortable clothing. Although they may seem laid back, they are in fact a bit vain about their appearance. They rarely sport any facial hair, and they may shave their heads rather than accept a receding hairline.

When he is feeling anxious or sad the Tree Elf generally either retreats into himself or becomes aggressively extroverted, seeking attention at all costs. In contrast to their public persona, Tree Elves are actually just a bit insecure and need lots of validation.

Although Tree Elves are less detached, more emotionally generous, and better at intimacy than most Urban Elves, and get even better as they age, there is a part of them that always seems elusive and distant, unable to fully commit to one creature. Most Trees have close, strong relationships with their mothers and more problematic ones with their dads. They understand and appreciate females deeply, but they may not have had the best male role model to show them how to sustain stable relationships. They tend to fear commitment, not because they secretly fear abandonment, like Urban Elves do, but because they have a strong need to feel free and unfettered. Before the age of forty, Tree Elves can have trouble with monogamy, but as they go through life they can evolve into loyal, loving mates.

Tree Elves tend to be artistic, and you can also sometimes find them in the field of the healing arts, working as massage therapists, chiropractors, acupuncturists, or other alternative medicine doctors.

They are emotionally devoted to their work and some can do quite well financially, but their refusal to conform may make it hard for them to establish successful careers. They may in turn feel frustrated and inadequate because of this. Tree Elves appear almost cavalier about money and like to express that the only work they can do is the kind that will not compromise their freedom. However, they have their share of insecurities about choosing a less conventional and dependable lifestyle. Their fears might have something to do with their ambiguous relationships with their not entirely dependable or assertive fathers.

I have two friends who fit into the Tree Elf category. One is a musician and works at a guitar shop. He's a loyal partner, although he likes to flirt innocently and connect deeply with many females. His energy is quite healing and comforting, without sexual overtones. He loves to hug his friends, massage their shoulders, and dance with them, albeit a bit awkwardly. Unlike the more squeamish Urban Elves, he likes camping and other outdoor activities. Bringing someone to the Burning Man Festival, where people camp out in the desert and create their own self-sustaining city, is his idea of the perfect vacation.

My other Tree Elf also loves outdoor festivals, music, dancing, and spirituality and likes to explore all the healing arts. He gets regular acupuncture treatments and attends sweat lodges and group meditations. We spent a day together doing yoga, eating brunch at an organic restaurant in a canyon, and visiting a puppy store.

"We can sniff puppies," he had told me happily.

I was a little surprised at the choice of words, but when we got there and held the wriggly, furry heartbeats in our hands and smelled their sweet baby scent, I understood what he meant.

After that he took me for a walk on the beach and a hike in the mountains where he showed me a mediation labyrinth he had made out of stones as well as a rock shaped like a vagina. (Tree elves are very interested in nature and sex and often relate the two, noticing and commenting on how plants or rocks can look sexual.) This Tree Elf planned the entire day, picked me up, drove speedily from location to location, and entertained me with an almost nonstop stream of wonderful stories. He wasn't as good a listener as an Urban Elf tends to be, but when I did find the space to say something he was always respectful and kind in his response.

A Tree Elf has the potential to turn into a Woodsman, the nurturing partner and caretaker. In fact, he probably thinks he *is* a Woodsman, but he's naturally a bit too scattered and complex to really qualify as this solid, if sometimes overly predictable (read: boring to a Banshee or Vamp), type.

This story tells it all: I was once having dinner with two other female Wood Nymphs and two male Tree Elves. I was telling them about each type and explaining how Woodsmen always make deep eye contact with you. As the Tree Elves listened, their eyes widened unconsciously. They looked into my eyes as I spoke. They were sure they were Woodsmen. But as soon as dinner was over they kissed and hugged us all warmly and dashed off into the night as Tree Elves do. A real Woodsman would be home with his love, tending the fire. However, he probably wouldn't have had as interesting a conversation over a bowl of miso, seaweed, and soba at a cool Japanese restaurant following a wild, sweaty night of expressive contact dance, improvising graceful and seductive moves with you.

Two of my serious boyfriends were Tree Elves. They matched me in sexual and creative energy, but they were young at the time and unstable in their careers. They weren't quite ready to settle down then, and even though I thought I was, Wood Nymphs also take their time to relax into stability. One Tree Elf made a particularly good partner for me, except that he couldn't satisfy my need to connect deeply at all times, a Wood Nymph trait that needs to be tempered. Tree Elves are naturally inclined to distribute their healing energy among a number of female creatures. If you're the jealous type (Wood Nymphs and Banshees, in particular), be on the look-out for this. You may have some work to do on your own in order to handle it. But remember, Tree Elves do have the capacity for true loyalty as they mature.

URBAN ELF *(Male)*: THE BRAIN

Urban Elves are technologically skilled and creative. You may discover them employed in the film industry, advertising, or other professions that involve technology and art. They are hard workers and can concentrate for long periods of time while sitting at a desk under fluorescent lights, although they have been known to complain about their nine-to-five office jobs and long for more creative expression. The more creative a field they are in, the happier they tend to be. An Urban Elf will usually make a decent living and is not bad with money, managing to pay his bills on time and enjoy a few of the finer things in life. They are usually stylish creatures with very specific and trend-conscious taste in clothes and accessories. Many of them like to use their clothes as disguises/masks, opting for cutting-edge, if not entirely flattering, eyewear and distracting, large shoes. In fact, a shaved head and sharp, rectangular glasses are the first clue that you might be in the presence of one of these guys, especially if they are carrying a laptop and a Starbucks cup. Although they will spend money on a good pair of glasses, they may not have much savings, and they worry about money enough that it can give them indigestion. Keep this in mind if they hesitate that extra moment when the bill comes. Not only are they anxious about their wallets; they also believe philosophically that female creatures are their equals and therefore might expect you to pay for yourself. Their philosophies are quite set, even rigid, and they try to live by them as much as possible.

A typical date with an Urban Elf involves a movie and chatting at a café about current events, the latest trends, politics, philosophy, and so on. He may not take you out to eat because he has a sensitive stomach (which explains the fact that Urban Elves are often quite slender) and is a bit private about his meal habits. Although Elves originated in the forest, the urban version is now quite removed from the natural world. Urbans avoid outdoor encounters, although if you can get one on a hike or to the beach, against their protestations, they may relax and reveal a different side to their personality. After all, Elves were born to be part of nature, and they really should return to it every once in a while.

However, if you are trying to meet an Urban Elf, you are more likely to encounter one, as the moniker suggests, in a coastal city rather than in the suburbs or rural inland states. Seek them out in a café rather than on a hike. Next time you go out for coffee look around; you'll probably be able to spot at least a few of these folks sitting at their laptops with their lattes. The personal habitat of the Urban is usually very clean and neat and well equipped with the latest technology. There may be a lyrical aspect to his world as well—an apartment building with a courtyard, flowers somewhere, romantic, natural lighting. After all, in spite of his adaptation to city life, this Elf is still connected to his roots in the woods.

Urban Elves in the bedroom are a romping, mischievous sort. They like to stay up all night playing—you have to keep up with them! But don't expect an Urban Elf to sleep over or make you breakfast; he prefers not to be seen in the harsh light of the day without his accessories and full get-up. Urbans often have trouble looking you directly in the eye (his cool glasses help him avoid this uncomfortable—for him—experience) or telling you that he thinks you are beautiful. The closest he usually comes is the word *cute*, which he uses to fit any situation, whether it's called for or not. Overt intimacy makes him feel awkward and he can go for years without a serious relationship. While he can be circumspect and calm about world events that might frighten others, the greatest fear of the Urban Elf may be abandonment. He has probably already experienced some form of this and is wary of having it happen again. Due to his extremely sensitive nature he has developed a façade of emotional detachment, although he can be kind and compassionate. He is also quite open to exploring different kinds of spirituality and can speak intelligently and deeply about spiritual matters. Just don't expect him to show you his true feelings for a long time. It may be hard to know him deeply, but if you are patient, he can be worth the wait.

The Urban Elf I dated was very shy and skittish at first. We had a lovely conversation that went on for hours, but it felt as if the time flew by. At the end of the evening, he gave me a quick kiss on the cheek and vanished into the night. On the next date he showed me his apartment, which was neat, tasteful, and sparsely furnished. He had a large collection of music, with an emphasis on classic artsy rock. He preferred the Flaming Lips, the Talking Heads, and R.E.M. His refrigerator was nearly empty. He had an impressive collection of stylish shoes, which were arranged in a perfect row by the door, to keep his floors clean. We made out, but he never took off his rectangular designer glasses. On the third date, we were in bed. He surprised me by his stamina and force, yet I sensed a certain emotional distance. When the date was over, he put on shoes and left his warm apartment to walk me to my car, but hugged me only quickly before vanishing again. He never called me, instead communicating only by text message or e-mail. I invited him to museums, concerts, parties, and dance events, but he always bowed out politely, preferring to spend his time with me in his own home. I never really knew what he was feeling. The idea of my kids seemed to make him nervous. In spite of this, I liked the Urban Elf very much. But I was still rebounding from my Satyr and was soon distracted by yet another Satyr; my relationship with the Elf fell away.

After the long-distance Satyr interest, whom I never actually met, stopped calling, I thought about the Elf and felt badly that I had pulled away from him. If he had been more communicative and if I had been more patient, we might have been a good match. He was sensitive, intelligent, and creative. We got along really well in bed. But after my trauma with the first Satyr, I both wanted and feared more immediate intimacy, and so I continued on my way.

GARDEN ELF:
THE PRETTY CREATURE

The Garden Elf is easily recognizable and thoroughly enjoys being identified by his type. He is always fit, impeccably groomed, and maintains a youthful appearance, even in late life. He is also always stylishly dressed, even if he's just running out for a latte at six in the morning. You will never witness a fashion faux pas on this Elf's svelte body, in spite of the style risks he takes, and he will be sure to notice any clothing mistake you might unwittingly make. He'll probably let you know about it, too, either directly or maybe in a more passive-aggressive way. He doesn't consider this rude, merely the helpful thing to do; as far as he's concerned, it would be like letting you walk around with food in your teeth! The Garden Elf's refined aesthetic extends to his environment as well, and he is usually interested in decorating his abode with care. He may like modern classics, Art Deco, 1950s retro, or Victorian, but whatever style he chooses will be displayed thoughtfully and tastefully. Like the Urban Elf, the Garden Elf tends to favor city environments because he needs to be in close proximity to culture and sophistication. However, as an Elf, his heart responds to nature and he must always have plants or flowers around him, even if it's just a window box of marigolds or a store-bought bouquet of sunflowers. He loves to receive flowers as a gift, but don't bring him carnations that have been dyed an unnatural color; he'll never let you forget it.

Garden Elves usually work in jobs that allow them to use their natural design talents and discriminating taste. They can be fashion designers, hairdressers, makeup artists, decorators, or work in retail. You can find them at art gallery openings discussing the latest trends over a glass of wine or at nightclubs dancing the night away with abandon. Some can also find themselves working in the performing arts. A certain type of young male heartthrob can fit into this category.

A date with a Garden Elf will usually involve some social activity, since they like to be around others, often to show you off as a couple. However, they are sensitive and can become easily irritated and are really at their best in a quiet environment. They may have many friends but are only close to a few. Their partner is usually their best and dearest friend. When things get romantic with a Garden Elf expect tenderness, attentiveness, and inspired, hot sex. However, they may remain slightly emotionally distant, not unlike their Urban counterparts.

As a parent, the Garden Elf is extremely conscientious and caring. He may choose not to have offspring for the simple reason that he knows how it may consume his life with worry, but if he overcomes this fear he will usually make an excellent, conscientious father.

Garden Elves can make great friends for any female type—they'll let you know how your hair really looks and what your best color is. They are also great to discuss relationships with. They can chat with you on the phone for hours when other types might balk at this. Satyrs, Centaurs, and Urban Elves usually hate being stuck on the phone with you, while Giants and Tree Elves will enjoy it, though not as much as Gardens. Their witty, sometimes acerbic sense of humor will keep you laughing, even if it might be at the expense of someone else.

The downside of the Garden Elf is that when he is feeling cranky or peeved he may lash out in a rather nasty way. It is important not to take these attacks too personally; the Garden Elf considers himself a fairly sensitive individual and will have trouble understanding why you are so offended by such an offhand remark. He is usually quick to forgive insults himself, so take a clue from him and let it go as soon as possible.

My Garden Elf friend was helping me shop for a vintage Chanel suit. He asked me my waist size and when I told him, he exclaimed, "Really?" in a horrified voice. I had recently given birth and was feeling a bit insecure about my middle. I took offense and told him so. This in turn insulted him, as he really hadn't meant any harm. He tried to make it up to me by sending me a *Buffy the Vampire Slayer* video, but I was so upset that it took me years to fully forgive him. Nymphs are not known for letting go of things easily, especially if the insult involves their physical appearance or sexuality. I ran into my Garden Elf at the market one day, and he was so charming and funny that I forgot I had been angry, and we have since become good friends once again.

WOODSMAN:
THE FAMILY CREATURE

Woodsmen can be kind and nurturing partners and good, solid fathers once they settle down. They are usually gainfully employed because, even if they are not wildly talented at what they do, other creatures like to be around them. Some may be narcissistic, especially in their early years, but not all are this way. One less alluring aspect of a Woodsman is that he can be overly conventional and boring for some types, especially Wood Nymphs, Banshees, and Vamps, who like more challenging mates. Pixies and Fairies, on the other hand, are drawn to him like moths to a lit candle.

Woodsmen tend to be a bit passive in terms of finding a mate, because they are used to being pursued. If you find one you like, don't be intimidated. Take a chance and approach him with confidence. You can assume that although he may have his share of attention, many female folk will avoid him entirely because they assume he is already attached. He likes bold, independent, optimistic females, and if he's not interested he won't be harsh in his rejection. In fact, he will let you down so gracefully that your ego will suffer only mild discomfort.

A true Woodsman will plan his date around you. He is comfortable in natural or urban environments, around crowds, or alone with the one he loves. Just graciously let him know what you like and let him accommodate your needs; he'll appreciate the opportunity.

Once captured and settled, a Woody will bring home the berries, make the fire, and read a bedtime story to the children before climbing in bed with you and enjoying a pleasant sexual encounter. It is possible for Woodsmen to get swept away by other aggressive creatures, so involving yourself with one of these is not for the faint of heart. However, the Woodsman's generally high self-esteem makes him less susceptible to seeking validation from lots of creatures, and once he finds his true love he is generally a very loyal partner.

Woodsmen are usually the products of fairly balanced homes, but they have their share of issues, like all the types. They may have had domineering fathers and narcissistic mothers, but in general they came into adulthood feeling loved and secure. Even if they had troubles at home, their personable manner keeps them surrounded by appreciative friends and acquaintances.

I have not dated any Woodsmen yet, but many of my friends have married them and started families. Although appealing in many ways, the Woodsman is by no means a perfect creature. He leaves his dirty socks in heaps around the bedroom. He attracts the attention of many female creatures, even when he's really not trying to. He refuses to talk about the book your book club is reading and hates museums. Although he spends a lot of time with the kids, he's not always the most responsible parent. He always manages to sneak in a boys' night out and leave you home with the kids, even when you really need some time to yourself.

In spite of these things, Woodsmen can be quite appealing. My favorite Woodsman friend can walk into a room and manage to make everyone feel happy with his warm, attentive banter. He once told me that he had heard on the news about a study that determined how happiness is contagious and can be passed on among people, even total strangers. This is a great thing for all types to remember.

If you are specifically seeking a Woodsman in order to start a family, remember that almost any of the other types, especially Tree Elves and Centaurs, can change into one under the proper circumstances. That said, don't count on this transformation, as it can lead you astray, and don't count on your relationship with this family man being trouble free. Woodsmen can seem overly self-centered or just plain boring to some types.

MERMAN: THE DUDE

Mermen are masculine, physically strong, and often emotionally protective. They are easy to be around due to their friendly, laid-back natures. Many tend to have liberal political views. They are not materialistic and can live happily on very little, as long as they have a surfboard and an ocean, a snowboard and a slope, or even a bicycle and an open trail nearby. On the downside, the Merman enjoys taking things easy so much that he may get lazy or overindulge in various substances. He also is so obsessed with his outdoor activities that he may neglect other aspects of his life. Water is usually the element that soothes and stimulates him most, but nature in general has a great allure for the Merman, and it can be hard for his partner to compete with it for his attention.

Mermen are easy to recognize in their casual, masculine, outdoorsy outfits. They often have a rugged appearance with skin that has been exposed to the elements and sun-bleached hair.

The Merman often comes from a supportive, kind family and has decent relationships with his parents. He also has plenty of friends, although he is still often regarded as a loner. He may choose to live on a houseboat, become a sailor and fisherman, or find a mountain cabin far from the city. He enjoys work that is physically active and not too intellectually or emotionally demanding—possibly making or repairing the equipment he relies on for his leisure activities.

Although he is smart and quite intuitive, he often chooses not to cultivate his intellect and intuition too deeply because he finds it agitating to sense so much of what other creatures are feeling. Instead, he may dull this part of himself with alcohol and marijuana. Sober Mermen may have a serious, if offbeat, spiritual practice.

Though they don't date as recklessly as Satyrs, Mermen are not particularly interested in settling down either, at least when they are young. When he does focus on partnering up, a Merman wants a strong, sexy mate who shares his interests. He is drawn to types who are athletically inclined and not particularly materialistic, but he appreciates a good dose of femininity as well. He is usually less attracted to the intellectual Urban Elf or to unpredictable, dark types like Vamps, Weregirls, or Banshees, and he can become restless around the less physically active Tess, but he admires the femininity and sex appeal of Nymphs, Fairies, Mermaids, Pixies, and Dryads and the physical strength and energy of Brownies.

Mermen make loving fathers, although they are not always the most stable or reliable types. They can be loyal but they can also get easily distracted. The same is true of them when it comes to friendships. They are well liked but sometimes don't uphold their side of a relationship, especially when distracted by alcohol or the charms of nature.

I had a huge crush on a Merman/Woodsman (or Waterwood) when I was a teenager. I met him at a dance club and he invited me and my friends to his party. It was a cookout on the beach, complete with tiki torches and kegs. We made out on the sand, and I was completely smitten with his bright smile, bleached hair, and athletic body. He even attended the prom with me and made quite an impression on all of the female creatures in my class. When I went away to college, I met a Faun whose gorgeous Pixie sister was dating this same Waterwood. They ended up getting married and having many equally gorgeous offspring. At the time I blamed myself for not being pretty enough, but of course our lack of success was based on something much less devastating than that—I was a Wood Nymph; she was a Pixie; he was a Waterwood. I wasn't really his type. They were made for each other.

I just hadn't learned the mythological dating system yet!

GIANT: THE GENTLE GUY

Giants are usually quite talented and successful in their chosen fields. They are generally financially stable and responsible. They excel in stimulating jobs that they enjoy. Giants can be scientists, writers, musicians, painters, directors, or even producers (although they are usually too introverted for that). They are well suited to working alone or with others and tend to have a few very close friends. Although he can be a bit introverted, the Giant is a natural host; he is a good cook or can at least barbecue well, choose the right bottle of wine, and generally create a lovely environment for his guests.

The home of a Giant is a cluttered but intriguing habitat, often in or near a culturally sophisticated city. Beautiful, if impractical, oddities fill every corner. Many Giants have spent much of their lives living alone and feel the need to create a nurturing environment that reflects their hidden feminine natures, especially if they fear they may never capture a Fairy to stay with them. Their collections may also be unconsciously intended as lures for female creatures—Fairies or Wood Nymphs in particular. The Giants' environments reflect their slightly eccentric but refined taste, which may not be apparent in the way they dress—they can be rather clueless about style and need the guidance of a Fairy to help them pull themselves together in that way.

The Giant enjoys food immensely—meat, sweets, and alcohol in particular. A date with a Giant almost always involves a good meal at a nice restaurant or his home. He may also take you to a play, reading, concert, or other cultural event. Giants like to go to out-of-the-way museums, antique stores, and second-hand bookstores. They love to collect books and usually have shelves overflowing with dusty volumes by authors ranging from Leo Tolstoy to Dr. Seuss.

Giants are not only avid readers; they also like to share personal stories about themselves, and they are good, attentive listeners. They can be quite gallant, a nearly lost art that many of the other types have not cultivated. However, if you don't return the affections of a Giant, he may pout mercilessly by the end of the evening.

Giants are passionate and loving creatures but they are not entirely comfortable in their bodies, so sex with them can be awkward and, at times, predictable. They will, however, be sure to look you in the eye, and they are comfortable saying things like, "You are beautiful," "I am falling in love with you," and "What can I do for you?"

The Giant is not typically interested in having children; he may prefer to give all of his attention to a partner (and to receive all of his partner's attention in return). If he finds himself in the role of a parent, a Giant will usually be very gentle and loving, if a bit bewildered by the responsibilities of parenthood.

Giants are much more emotionally vulnerable than they might appear, so keep this in mind if one starts behaving in a slightly harsh way toward you. They will rarely be overtly mean, but they may express passive aggression in subtle ways if their feelings have been hurt. They tend toward depression more than anger and will most likely pull into themselves if they are upset. A happy, secure Giant is a pleasure to be around. He will shower you with gifts and make sure your needs are well met.

My dating experiences with Giants were positive but ultimately frustrating for both of us. The first Giant I dated took me to a lovely dinner on a canyon garden patio strewn with rose petals and Christmas lights where he ate large amounts of meat and sugar and finished off a whole bottle of wine by himself. At his home, filled with paintings of mythological creatures and polished chunks of rose quartz and jade, he played wonderful music by angry female artists and gave me some of the beautiful photographs he had taken and trinkets he had found. I was charmed and felt safe in his presence. However, in the bedroom, Giants are often a bit slow and self-conscious, while Wood Nymphs are . . . well . . . Nymphs. Things didn't go as well as we would have liked, and by morning, I had a grumpy Giant lying on his back beside me, glaring at the ceiling. I still have warm feelings for this Giant, however. I know he'll make a wonderful partner and husband for the right creature.

The second Giant arrived at our coffee date with a huge box of dusty items he had gathered from his cluttered home. There was a taxidermist's vampire bat in a glass box, a day-by-day astrology guide for both of our signs, a pet rock, an umbrella, a book about centaurs, a DVD of a film he had made, a mix tape of music, a C-3PO doll, and more. When we were getting coffee, I dropped something out of my purse and the gallant Giant swooped to retrieve it. There was an awkward moment when we both realized it was a thin menstrual pad, but he immediately put me at ease with a joke, exclaiming. "What a tiny handkerchief, m'lady!" We had an interesting date during which he gave me suggestions about my career and finances in a nurturing way. However, the chemistry wasn't entirely there, and I was a bit overwhelmed by the gifts. We ended the date feeling affectionate toward each other, but both knowing we wouldn't be seeing each other in this way again.

I have a Giant friend who lives alone in a beautiful house with a romantic garden. He works at an office job but spends a great deal of time writing science fiction stories on an old typewriter, taking lovely photographs, and playing his guitar. He has a lot of online female friends who tend to confess their sadness to him and he is always compassionate, although sometimes the sorrow of others can overwhelm him. Giants must be aware of this tendency to attract needy individuals and find ways to protect themselves from being pulled down by these needs.

SATYR: MR. SEX

Satyrs are perhaps one of the most alluring but challenging of the forest folk. One can sometimes recognize them by their intense gaze and lean, athletic bodies. They often sport goatees and tattoos. Sometimes they will wear their hair in attention-grabbing styles, such as dreadlocks or Mohawks. Their clothes can be casual or very style-conscious, but whatever they wear is thought out and intended to attract. Even jeans and a T-shirt are carefully selected—the right cut of the jeans, the right logo on the shirt—to say "sexy and cool."

Satyrs are graceful, quiet, and composed but can become extroverted after a few drinks or perhaps a hit of pot, both of which they enjoy. Even when sober, one always senses a rumbling beneath the surface. Their sensual energy gyrates through them, and when it is released, watch out. But don't expect to tie one of these creatures down. Satyrs are sexually seductive to an extreme degree. They know exactly what they want in the bedroom and how to get it. Beware these forest folk if you are looking to settle down in a nice cottage for the long haul, but play with them if you are bored, lonely, and secure enough to handle it when they inevitably run off along the woodland path.

Most of the Satyr's lifestyle has unconsciously developed around sexual satisfaction. They may gravitate toward certain professions that provide access to potential partners. Many Satyrs are rock musicians, actors, or athletes, although photographers and artists sometimes fall into this category as well. They will pick their cars, clothing, hairstyle, music, and even what they read, watch, and eat with the conscious or unconscious idea that it may attract more partners, as well as to satisfy their sensual natures. Whatever their budget, their living environments place tremendous emphasis on a large, comfortable bed, usually with a headboard that can be used for leverage while having sex, and the biggest computer, TV, and sound system they can afford. They usually have small kitchens and well-stocked liquor cabinets. Graphic art may decorate their walls. But although Satyrs can appear quite stylish, they are so consumed by conquering others sexually that, aside from their innate sensuality, they may not know what their actual taste is anymore. The thing that is most confusing about Satyrs is how they can convince you, and themselves, that their feelings for you are deep and not just sexual. They can say things like "I love you," easily and without compunction. They really believe it at the time, so it can be quite convincing, especially to the less cynical, more gullible types, like Dryads, or to any type that tends to be more insecure, like Wood Nymphs. All of this predatory behavior is really just a defense against what a Satyr says he needs but really fears most—space. He will use the excuse of "needing space" (he actually uses these clichéd words) to move from one mate to the next, or push loved ones away with harsh behavior, when in truth he is terrified of aging and being left alone. He responds to feelings of stress, sadness, and even excitement by seeking the next creature to ravish rather than stopping to examine his deep feelings.

You can find Satyrs at rock concerts, skateboard parks, sporting events, movie premieres—anywhere there is excitement and a crowd of attractive creatures. A perfect Satyr date? It really doesn't matter to him what you do as long as you end up where he ultimately wants to be—in bed.

My assessment of this type may sound harsh, but Satyrs do have some very appealing qualities. Some can make devoted fathers, as they see their children as direct extensions of themselves, and their natural narcissism encourages an attentive, if somewhat indulgent parenting style. They are usually too selfish to make very devoted friends but are always interesting and even exciting guests at parties. Sometimes they will bond closely with one or two other Satyrs with whom they can commiserate over the neediness of Wood Nymphs and the emotionality of Banshees. As lovers, they can be so charming, sensual, and seductive that whatever pain they put you through may be worth it. Things can work out if you remain conscious and do not expect to get something out of the relationship that they are usually incapable of providing. There is also the chance that they may evolve into a more stable combination type, but it can be dangerous to count on this. If you expect it to happen and try to force it, you may be in for a big disappointment and a lot of pain.

I became infatuated with a Satyr who danced wildly with me and then, as the music slowed, stood in front of me, wrapped my arms around him, and placed my hand on his pounding heart. We stood that way for a long time, and when it was over I had a hard time shaking the experience (Wood Nymphs and Dryads in particular respond powerfully to gestures like this). I thought it meant more than the Satyr thought it did; he was just being true to his nature. A genuine Satyr, or even an immature Tree Elf, may never understand the effect he has. "It's not like I put her hand on my pounding cock!" he would say to himself, feeling perfectly justified about the whole thing.

After I dated the Urban Elf, I had an e-mail correspondence with a Satyr who lived out of state. He sent me poetry, music videos, and nude pictures of himself, including one of his muscular rear end, and one of his feet, about which he happened to be very vain. He was passionate and enthusiastic, calling and texting me all through the day and late at night. This Satyr promised to visit me but then dropped out of the picture entirely. When I finally reached him, days before his intended visit, I asked whether he had met someone new. He admitted that he had, we talked for a minute more, then hung up and that was the end of it. Satyrs hate conflict and will cut you out of their lives entirely when they are finished with you.

My second Internet Satyr was in his mid-fifties, and in spite of his deceptive goatee and tattoos, had matured past much of the typical young Satyr drama. On our first date, he invited me to dinner at a sushi bar with a group of his friends. Everyone got drunk on sake and gobbled down raw fish. The Satyr flirted with me mercilessly, but when I flirted back in an e-mail the next day, he told me that he was wary of lust, because it only leads to pain, and that he was simply looking for a friend. I visited him once more at his home with a gym, a screening room, and a bright red bathroom. There were Sharpie markers in a cup by the toilet so the guests could scribble their graffiti on the walls. I shivered with cold through a bad Chinese film. As I was saying good-bye, the coat rack fell on top of me. The Satyr said, "I wonder if that is a sign." We e-mailed a few times more but nothing came of it. Because this Satyr had learned to control his sexual impulses (at least until he found a female creature who appealed to him more—I learned he was dating a very young Pixie a few months later), there wasn't much left for us to do together, but I am grateful to him for sparing me the pain he so correctly alluded to.

My Satyr boyfriend, the one who preceded all of my Internet

dating, was fun for a year, until one night, at on outdoor concert, another Nymph started shaking her booty at him. He engaged with her and ignored me. My Nymph nature wanted to tell her to back off and pull him away, but I controlled myself and gently put my hand on his arm. When he continued to ignore me, I got very upset and said I was going home. He replied with a cold good-bye. I was under tremendous stress at the time, trying to buy a house (Nymphs like the security of a pretty abode with trees, flowers, and water around it), so I overreacted, even for my type. I fell crying into the arms of my friends, a Fairy, a Mermaid, and a Dryad. They consoled me and told me not to approach him until I was calm. Luckily I wasn't being counseled by another Nymph or a Banshee, who would probably have told me to go tell him and his new dance partner to fuck off. When I was calm, I went over to my Satyr to hug him and say a nice good-bye. He held me at arm's length and spoke in a cold voice: "I thought you had left already." That was basically the end of our relationship. When I look back at it, it was traumatic at the time, but now I understand that it is a rather run-of-the-mill occurrence between a Wood Nymph and Satyr. A Satyr may not be the one who looks mad or upset, but he thrives on this kind of drama nonetheless.

HOB: MR. SAVVY

These forest friends are clever and often quite successful in their careers. Finance, law, and real estate are all fields that appeal to Hobs and in which they generally excel. They are usually clean-cut and dress in conventional business attire or neat casual clothing. They often walk quickly and have rather loud voices. They

live in pleasant environments and enjoy what life has to offer, although their work and drive to get ahead can consume them and keep them from fully appreciating the moment. Although they are quite disciplined on the job, they are less so when it comes to exercise and eating. Hobs would rather skip the treadmill and relax with some chocolate after a long day at the office, but their perfectionism keeps them fairly diligent.

In spite of his focus on his work, the Hob also values the idea of family and can be a very involved parent. Although Hobs are sometimes controlling, they truly love their offspring and would do almost anything for them. They are selective about their friendships but are similarly devoted to their closest friends.

Hobs hide their sensitive natures under an abrasive, slightly sarcastic persona that may be off-putting to others but can get them what they want in the professional world. When a Hob feels anxious he can be quite rude and insulting. Sometimes he will insult you so unconsciously that if you bring it up to him he will be genuinely shocked, believing he was being supportive. In fact, he will interpret the fact that you took offense as an offense to him and you may become engaged in a bitter dispute. Many Hobs had difficult relationships with their mothers, and they can be mistrustful of females in general. They may devote a good deal of time to complaining about how they were treated as children. If they felt misunderstood, unseen, and insulted they may spend their adult lives trying to make up for these feelings. This self-awareness is a positive trait, but it can become a bit indulgent. Some Hobs can never overcome their issues of low self-esteem and will repeatedly act out on their partners in harsh, judgmental, and sarcastic ways. But if your Hob feels nurtured he will make you laugh with his clever remarks and can be a loyal partner and a good provider. He is also much more romantic than he appears to be and knows the value of greeting cards, flowers, and, of course, a box of chocolates.

If you are very drawn to a Hob, try meeting him for some fun, outdoor activity like a walk on the beach. Food-centered dates are also good, although the Hob may spend a lot of time talking about his weight and health or, quite possibly, yours!

Two of my dates with Hobs were brief. They kept their sunglasses on for the first few minutes and cracked nervous jokes. They both complained about their mothers who did not give them the acceptance and affection they needed when they were children. When it was time to leave, both gave me friendly but anxious hugs and darted off, with no mention of connecting again in the future.

Another Hob was harsh and even combative on the phone, bantering with me sarcastically, but when we met in person he was quite generous and nurturing. He graciously let me pick the restaurant, paid for the dinner, and then bought a carton of chocolate ice cream to share with me in my kitchen.

I felt comfortable with this Hob and told him a story about a spiritual experience I had, in which my father seemed to appear to me as a white horse on the day of his death. The Hob tried to argue that there is nothing after death.

"That's the beauty of it," he said. "That all we have is now."

I appreciated this last sentiment but still felt he had dismissed me harshly, and my Nymphish feelings were hurt. We argued a little, until he stopped and took my wrists in his hands.

"They're so little," he said gently, fondling them.

For a moment I realized I cared less about what type he was or even about his spiritual beliefs, and more about this feeling of connection that I so longed for. However, when he came back the next day to take me to a museum, he was rather grumpy and sarcastic. He told me I looked tired, once again hurting my feelings. He chastised me for not knowing a fact about a popular musician. Alas, in spite of our sweet moment of connection, this, too, was not meant to be.

FAUN: THE ETERNAL YOUTH

Fauns are fairly shy but can also be outgoing, especially after a few drinks, which they enjoy. In fact, all the sensual pleasures, including eating, drinking, and kissing, delight them; however, they are prone to addictive behavior and need to watch themselves. On the upside of this, Fauns can be very disciplined when they set their minds to something and are able to give up their addictions, or at least replace them with healthier ones like exercising. They tend to be a bit vain,  which leads them to work out quite religiously, watch what they eat, and put a good deal of attention into their grooming habits. Their clean-shaven faces and use of quality moisturizer can give them a youthful appearance. They are generally rather creative, although somewhat lazy. Another interesting fact about Fauns is that they seem to be fairly passive, but when angered or upset they can be aggressively withdrawn or just plain aggressive until they get their way. Their stubborn nature is not obvious at first. Fauns are playful, romping companions, and can express affection toward both males and females; however, they may be less interested in sex. They may make up for this with their cute appearance and sweet nature, depending on what is important to you, of course.

Fauns aren't usually particularly career oriented and they may be a bit lost as to what they want to do when they "grow up," no matter how old they are. They may choose jobs as personal trainers, coaches, or professional waiters so that they can enjoy physical activity and sunshine (they are happiest in warm climates) and avoid demanding nine-to-five office jobs under less flattering fluorescent lights. Sometimes these freer schedules allow them to pursue more creative exploits. Luckily, Fauns are not particularly materialistic and don't feel the same need to attract others with their possessions, the way Satyrs do, so their less lucrative career choices, if enjoyable enough, are satisfying for them. It is imperative that they avoid stressful situations because this will often lead to addictions if they turn to substances as a way to comfort themselves.

Because Fauns don't need too many material comforts, relying more on sensual and emotional ones, they are satisfied living in small spaces, as long as they have their coffeemaker, smoothie blender, TV, DVD player, running shoes, and weights. They dress in casual, sporty attire, but they are conscious about maintaining a neat and up-to-date look. Most don't own a suit or a tie, and if they do, they reserve them for special occasions. They love the attention they get from these rare shows of elegance.

Fauns can be surprisingly good fathers due to their ability to identify with their child-selves. However, they are a little less skilled at romantic relationships due to their sexual ambiguity and the fact that intimacy of that kind makes them feel vulnerable. Unlike Tree Elves, they do not like to discuss their personal issues, although they are much better listeners than Trees. They often prefer to be alone and can easily become quite isolated. The Faun's fears are less about loneliness than about getting older. Sometimes this encourages rather selfish behaviors on their part as they devote much time and energy to looking and feeling young.

My Faun date was generally quite sweet. He treated me kindly and was attentive to my emotional and physical needs, although he was a bit financially challenged, as many Fauns tend to be. Our main troubles took place in the bedroom. Although he was an incredibly generous lover (not unusual for his type), the Faun had trouble fulfilling his own sexual needs with a partner in the room and did better by himself. This caused great tension, mostly on my end, as Wood Nymphs unfortunately get a large degree of their self-esteem through their sexuality and being able to satisfy their partners.

Fauns make great male companions. They can be as sensitive and attentive as female friends. They notice hairstyles and mood changes and listen as you discuss the nuances of relationships or physical ailments. At the same time, they can be quite masculine and protective. Although I am not well suited to romantic involvement with Fauns, I value their friendship and support.

VAMPIRE: THE PROVOCATEUR

Some creatures like to emphasize their type rather than downplay it. While Fauns are more comfortable blending in and Werewolves actively try to hide certain parts of their personality, some types, like Satyrs, Garden Elves, Tree Elves, and Urban Elves, enjoy showing off their type with their hairstyles, the way they dress, and the general way they behave in public situations.

Vampires are particularly proud of their type. Like Satyrs, they are rather narcissistic and do not worry about frightening away potential dates with their reputation. The difference is that the Satyr honestly does not believe there is anything to avoid about his type, while the Vampire revels in the dangerous mythology that precedes him.

Everything a Vampire does reflects his mythology. He chooses to live in dramatic, eccentric environments. Even if he does not have a lot of resources he will use his ingenuity to create a mysterious mood. He likes employment that is at least somewhat glamorous, but if he can't find his dream job he'll take work in a photo lab or dark restaurant, anywhere the sun doesn't shine too brightly. He wears somewhat dramatic clothing, usually black, and isn't afraid of an ostentatious hairstyle or tattoo. He makes a point of listening to extreme music, watching horror movies and reading dark fantasy fiction, and letting you know about it. In bed he generally likes to experiment with classic kink (think handcuffs, dog collars, and cross-dressing), even if he'd be just as happy with a more "vanilla" encounter. If he throws in a little bondage and dress-up he is maintaining his reputation as a cutting-edge type.

With Vampires more than others, it may be hard to detect the individual creature beneath the archetype. They have usually formed their personas as a way to disguise any vulnerability in their psyches. Many of them have been raised in conservative, middle-class families that do not understand or appreciate their eccentric, creative natures. Because most of them tend to be introverts at heart, despite their penchant for the performing arts, they have used their physical appearance and work to demonstrate their rebellious nature rather than to rebel in a more active way as Satyrs tend to do.

I have rarely seen a Vampire firsthand in the active role of father or even husband, although there are some who have done this successfully. However, the Vampire tends to put his artistic interests, his image, and his romantic obsessions above the responsibilities of conventional relationships. As he matures he may settle down with the objects of his heart's desire and maintain the romance for many years, as the surrealist artist Salvador Dalí did with his wife, Gala. A Vampire may also choose to father a child and can be a doting parent, although he is rarely interested in large broods of offspring that will take him away from his other interests.

I met a Vampire at a café on a sunny day. He kept his shades on most of the time and seemed irritated by the light. He had prominent eyeteeth; very pale, ageless skin; and rather ruddy lips, almost as if he wore lipstick. The picture he had used on his online profile had been taken ten years before, and even though he had not aged that much, he had appeared much more attractive in the shot than in real life. We spoke about Jean Cocteau, Tim Burton, and Dead Can Dance. He told me about his work as an assistant cameraman on various interesting projects. Vampires have sophisticated taste in the arts, and this intrigued me. However, he was somewhat disconnected emotionally. He did not meet my gaze, laughed nervously, and fidgeted throughout the meeting. Although he paid for my tea, he made an irritated face when he received the check. He told me rather proudly that he had been addicted to various substances and still smoked cigarettes. I could smell them on him and they had stained his teeth. He had long, pale hands and long, sharp fingernails that gave me a queasy feeling. All in all, I was sure this wasn't the right match for me, and we went our separate ways with a sigh of relief.

WEREWOLF: THE ENGIMA

Werewolves are usually quite charming and attractive, if a bit shy. It is easy to mistake one for a Faun, although they are more rugged in appearance. They are intelligent and well read. They stay well informed about the state of the world. You can engage in long, interesting conversations with them, and they are good at coming up with entertaining ways to spend time with you. A Werewolf is a night creature and is familiar with all of the best bars, restaurants, and nightclubs. They usually hold steady jobs in offices or other relatively quiet environments. This work pays their rent, although their homes are often small and cramped. Werewolves dress with some offbeat style. They tend to shop at thrift shops and turn up their noses at conventional stores. Typical Werewolf attire consists of blue jeans, a button-down shirt over a T-shirt, heavy shoes or boots, some kind of cool coat, and possibly a fedora or other interesting hat.

These creatures are able to maintain friendships and have a lot of casual acquaintances to party with, although they rarely let anyone get too close to them. If you do get close to one he will be affectionate and even worshipful in his behavior . . . for a time. However, the trouble starts when Werewolves allow themselves to abuse drugs or alcohol. Because of their loner personalities, their high-strung natures, and propensity for hanging out at bars and parties, they have frequent opportunities to overindulge. When this occurs, their personalities change so suddenly you may not see it coming. Some Werewolves can even change without substance abuse. You may be having a perfectly pleasant conversation with one when he will suddenly snap out about something that seems insignificant. For instance, Werewolves can easily get impatient with creatures who are less informed than they are. They can become irritated by any small sign of weakness. They can also interpret a perfectly innocent statement as an insult. Be sure to use caution around Werewolves. If you do decide to become involved with one of them, you will have to put up with a lot of challenges. It is not impossible to overcome these, however.

If a Werewolf gets upset, try to speak calmly and rationally to him. Reassure him that you were not trying to insult him, and try not to take what he says personally. Stick to the facts of the situation rather than bringing in any emotional subtext. I can best illustrate the Werewolf with a story.

I met my Werewolf date at a funky café. His hair was graying, he had a bit of facial hair, and his face was quite handsome. He wore a long, black wool coat and battered shoes.

The Werewolf had a soft, well-modulated voice and kept a respectful distance from me. He admired the photos of my kids in my wallet. He seemed slightly disoriented and explained that he was just waking up, since he usually worked all night and slept during the day. As he rambled on about obscure lounge acts, experimental film, and his art projects, I decided to invite him to a party I was going to later that night. He asked whether I would feel more comfortable meeting him there or driving us, and I decided to drive, since he seemed charming and harmless.

On the way to the party, the Werewolf directed me politely; he knew the night streets quite well. He spoke a little about his childhood, confessing nervously that he had been raised as a strict Mormon (potentially quite traumatic for a Werewolf, but I didn't yet know he was one) and although he had rejected the religion, the principles still weighed heavily on him. He also asked me a lot of questions about my writing and experiences as a parent. This impressed me, especially because Satyrs and Centaurs, the two types I had recently found myself most attracted to, are rather self-involved and rarely inquire about these things.

When we arrived at the party, a bohemian hipster affair in the backyard of a charming 1940s house, the Werewolf began to drink. The first drink made him flirtatious. The second drink made him outgoing with my friends. By the third drink, he was engaged with a brilliant, famous, feisty Mermaid. They ignored my attempts to join in the conversation. By the time we were ready to leave, the Werewolf's facial hair had suddenly sprouted and he looked wild-eyed and unkempt. He snapped at me as I drove, telling me rudely that I was taking the long way home. When I lightly commented that he was being bossy, he seemed to become even more tense.

"I need to eat something," he growled, so we stopped at a late-night Indian restaurant. I was hesitant to continue the evening, but I was worried about refusing him and also curious about his type (in spite of his sudden hirsuteness, I still hadn't figured him out).

He wolfed down curries, chicken tikka, and naan, then snarled that he had forgotten his credit card, so I had to pay. He also made sure to get all the leftovers to go and didn't offer me any.

While he ate, he told me about his last girlfriend, who had accused him of becoming judgmental and rude like her father. She didn't understand how his personality could change so much, and he had insisted that he hadn't changed at all; she was just projecting her father issues onto him.

On the way home I was still curious about what type he was and began to question him as casually as possible. I asked him why he had replied "prefer not to say" to the question about taking drugs on the Internet dating profile, as this response to any question always caught my attention and seemed like a bit of a red flag. He looked irritated and I wished I hadn't asked.

I said, "Oh, you know, I was just wondering if you smoke pot."

"I was on prescription drugs for a while," he said in a menacing tone, and I dropped the subject.

We got back to the café, where he'd left his car, late at night. I held out my hand to shake his, but the Werewolf surprisingly hugged me instead, then got out of my car and fled into the night.

I was actually quite relieved when he did not contact me again. You could say I got off easily. I don't know what might have happened if the moon were full, and even in the name of research, I don't care to find out.

On a side note, I did run into him months later shopping at a high-priced natural foods market. He looked quite bewildered, handsome, and innocent in his short-sleeved button-down shirt and glasses. I would never have guessed at his darker side. He didn't seem to notice me, but I thought he was just pretending not to see me, as I was doing with him.

When I got home I sent him an e-mail apologizing for not coming up and greeting him. He replied saying I should have, and joked that I could have explained to him why everything cost twice as much as where he usually shopped (hence his bewildered expression).

I dated one Werewolf for a considerable period of time, but I mistook him for a Tree Elf type until very recently because he loved nature and music from the 1960s. However, his mood swings, his edgy style, and his fondness for alcohol and playing music all night long are signs of the Wolf. One night he exploded in anger, calling me names and lunging at me. I broke up with him then and there and didn't speak to him for years, but we have since become casual friends. He is a devoted father and loyal, loving friend to the people who accept him for who he is. My Nymph nature is such that I am apt to try to change the Werewolves who come into my life. This never works.

As mentioned, Werewolves are usually charming, creative, and attractive until any kind of substance is introduced into the picture, or, in some cases, until they are triggered emotionally by something. If they get the right help and support, their human compassion can triumph over their animal nature and they will be caring, if eccentric, partners for the right Weregirl, Fairy, or Dryad. They may also change into Fauns, Tree Elves, or Woodsmen over time.

Female Types

WOOD NYMPH: THE ARTIST

These highly sexual females are also emotionally intense. They love to move their bodies as much as possible, to relieve the considerable tension they feel, but also enjoy intellectual stimulation and are often quite literary. They generally work in the arts or in a fairly nontaxing job that will allow them to pursue their artistic interest at the same time. Wood Nymphs usually have longish hair that tangles easily, and graceful, youthful bodies that they like to dress in diaphanous, provocative clothing. Their favorite outfits are tight yoga pants or jeans with flowing blouses. Wood Nymphs are completely uninhibited on the dance floor and in bed. All life's sensual pleasures are important to her. She loves music, soft textures, vibrant colors, the scent of flowers, the tastes of exotic foods. In spite of her interest in materialism for sensuality's sake, she would rather live in a plain, rented room and eat rice and lentils every day than have to sacrifice love or creative work.

Not every male creature can handle a Wood Nymph. Her passions run hot, both sexually and when she is angered. Her relationship with her family, especially her father, is often quite close, intense, and problematic. She's restless in the bedroom and demands even more attention out of it. She tends to be jealous and easily wounded and then she may stray. However, once she feels loved, a Wood Nymph will shower you with affection, sex, poetry, flowers, and cake.

Wood Nymphs thrive when they realize that they are a bit high maintenance and do what has to be done to take care of themselves. Therapy is often helpful to them, as long as they choose a caring, sane counselor since these Nymphs can be self-destructive and unconsciously drawn to forest folk who do not serve them well, both in their business and in their personal life. Creative expression is also helpful for Nymphs. It is a way for them to heal themselves on a profound level and may also be how they make their living.

I have a few Wood Nymph friends but not many, as we tend to annoy each other with our sensitivity and emotionality.

DRYAD: NATURE CREATURE

The Dryad, or Tree Nymph, is a very attractive, natural, feminine creature with great healing abilities. Many counselors and massage therapists fall into this category, as they love to help others as much as possible. Dryads often wear flowing, graceful, not particularly revealing clothing. Their favorite color may be purple, and they also like to wear blues, greens, and whites, often layered together. They enjoy yoga classes, modern dance, vegetarian cooking and dining, gardening, and the arts. A Dryad makes a wonderful companion. She is self-aware and thoughtful. She will gracefully admit, "That's my stuff," in an argument; after some experience with psychotherapy she is probably able to identify when her own issues are contributing to a problem in a relationship. The trouble with Dryads is that they can become depressed. They may turn to substance abuse, especially as young Nymphs. When this happens, the Dryad needs a lot of patience and love to help her recover.

Dryads can come from challenging family situations. Their relationships with their parents are sometimes complex, and their healing natures have often been developed in response to some need to repair emotional issues in the home. They make excellent, if a bit overprotective, mothers themselves, and they are able to maintain close, loving connections with their partners. They do tremendous amounts of work on themselves and value others who are willing to do the same. A good companion for the Dryad is the Tree Elf, as they share a creative drive and a desire to nurture others.

If you are dating a Dryad, take her on a hike, to a yoga class, or out for a healthy, organic meal. She will enjoy listening to you talk about yourself and will provide gentle insights into every topic. Be careful not to take advantage of her giving nature and try to reciprocate as much as possible. A long-term relationship with a Dryad can be very rewarding, especially if she is nurtured as much as she tends to nurture others.

I seek the help of Dryads when I need to be comforted or healed. One of my favorite Dryads is a healer in her sixties. My yoga teacher, veterinarian, and dermatologist are also Dryads.

Where would I be without them?

URBAN ELF *(Female)*:
THE SMARTY PANTS

Female Elves of this type like to live in cities and are often librarians, editors, teachers, writers, or other rather literary academics. They may also be involved in visual arts, and they love postmodern bands and alternative music in general. To express their intelligent, innovative, quirky personality, they may don small, funky eyeglasses, dowdy-hip attire, possibly involving a blouse, a vintage cardigan, a skirt, knee-socks and loafers or Mary Janes, and a hairstyle chosen for cool appeal rather than what might be most flattering (short, blunt bangs are popular). When they like you, they will make you a CD mix with a bit of orchestral pop, a bit of art rock, and something surprising. Their nervous systems are hardier than those of the male Urban Elf and they tend to have less discipline, so they may be smokers and prefer candy for dinner rather than soup (a male Urban favorite). Exercise is not a favorite activity for them but they get enough from just walking around the cities where they dwell. They drink a lot of coffee in cafés and rarely leave their local Starbucks without a pastry. If single, they will eat dinner alone in their apartments in urban bohemian areas, often accompanied by a cat. As an independent type, the Urban Elf knows how to fix things and support herself. Like the male Urban Elf, this female version is a bit standoffish. This may stem from an upbringing in which strong displays of emotion were discouraged. Although kind and devoted, the Urban Elf's parents were probably strict and not particularly effusive. In turn, their daughter is often reserved and can appear cool or even cold, but her true nature is more complex than this. Get close to an Urban Elf and you will find the passionate, almost Nymph-like persona that lurks within. Until a female Elf fully acknowledges her wilder side, she may continually get involved with unsuitable Satyrs who express this passion for her. Because she depends on them to do this, she may lose sight of herself and risk having her heart broken. It is best for the Urban Elf to embrace her wilder side, even while maintaining a buttoned-up, introverted persona in the world. When she accepts her inner wilderness, she will easily attract a loving partner who appreciates all sides of her nature and who gives her more than just the companionship and compatibility she says she wants. After all, the secret wish of the Urban Elf is to have a romance bursting with passion.

She can be the perfect match for the male Urban Elf if they learn to see through each other's cool façades to the true warmth that lies beneath or help each other to bring this aspect of their personalities out into the light.

I meet many Urban Elves in my field as a writer, as they are drawn to publishing. I find them to be loyal, trustworthy, and highly intelligent. They always know the answer to literary questions and make excellent teachers and editors. In their delicate eyewear, skirts, and flats they are always tastefully put together. Classic Urban Elf females may not always open up at first, but after a while they often surprise me by reaching out in unexpectedly warm ways such as sending sweet notes on old-fashioned floral stationery or bringing over delicious home-cooked dishes.

FAIRY: THE FEMME

Often fair-haired (by nature or a nurturing bottle) and slight of build (due to her tendency to move at a quick pace), the Fairy enchants with her quirky personality, flitty grace, and generous, if somewhat capricious, nature. Don't make her mad, however; these forest folk are sensitive and have quick tempers. But they will recover their positive attitude soon enough. Fairies like to stay in shape but can get bored easily, so they usually need a fashion magazine or at least an iPod to get them through their workout. Although they love to eat, they are generally careful about the calories they consume and will opt for a salad and sushi over a steak anytime. They do love dessert, however, and will cut out that extra slice of bread so they can have an extra-large frozen yogurt or other low-calorie sweet treat. Fairies get their hair cut and colored on a regular basis and stay up to date with manicures, pedicures, facials, and waxing. Makeup is important to them and they apply it lightly but impeccably. They enjoy shopping and are usually fashion conscious, with an offbeat style. They always know how to put things together in unique and attractive ways. A typical outfit for a Fairy is a silk blouse, good blue jeans, and fabulous high heels, or a silk slip dress with ballet flats. They collect shoes passionately, and their closets and drawers overflow with the sparkling treasures that they cherish. Fairies tend to gravitate toward jobs in fashion and design. You can seduce them with pretty things and pretty words, but that will only get you so far, as they require true emotional fulfillment in addition to superficial romance. They are emotional caretakers and will gladly spend hours processing feelings with you. Still, there is always something vaguely distant about Fairies. Even the creatures closest to them sense this and can become frustrated by it. It is also what makes these forest folk so alluring to many. When a Fairy likes you, or even loves you, she won't easily let you know the extent of her feelings. Once in a while she can get carried away and behave almost like a Nymph in her ardor, but this is an exception to the rule.

Fairies usually have positive relationships with their mothers and make loyal girlfriends and good mothers themselves, if they choose to settle down. They generally come from stable homes and are in turn able to cultivate a pleasant environment for themselves and their families. Like Nymphs, they love to be surrounded by fresh flowers, pleasing textures, and soft, soothing colors. Although they enjoy nature they are not as comfortable in it as Dryads. They prefer relaxing with a lemonade on a chaise in a well-tended garden to camping in the woods.

I have a Fairy friend who gives me facials. She lives in an apartment filled with pretty things and decorated in creams and light greens. She has a silver crescent moon, a bust of David, and a wrought iron cande-labra in her courtyard. She wears pink cashmere sweatpants, satin camisoles, and silver shoes. She is sexy but shy, strong but soft, loving but somewhat reserved at first. As a Wood Nymph, I get along with her very well. However, if she is in a bad mood she will occasionally lash out. Luckily, she always calls herself on it, usually right away.

PIXIE: MISS POPULARITY

Pixies are similar to Fairies, but they are a bit less intensely feminine and more prag-matic in style and mannerisms. Although fashion conscious, they place less emphasis on image and more on relationships. They are confident, cheerful, and easygoing and are less easily inflamed than their Fairy sisters.

The Pixie is usually quite competent in her chosen field. There are many celebrity Pixies, as this extroverted, social type tends to make an excellent actress. Her likeable, upbeat nature serves her well in the work arena as well as in her personal life.

A Pixie is a good friend to have. She's supportive, thoughtful, and a good listener. These abilities stem from a childhood that was usually quite positive. She is often the favored offspring of loving parents and has close relationships with her siblings. Her circle of friends is always growing. Her closest friendships are with Fairies and Dryads. She can work well in business relationships with Hobbies. Brownies and Wood Nymphs tend to envy her and consider her boring simultane-ously. Vamps, Weregirls, and Banshees are too dark to make very good companions for this lighthearted (*they* might say light-headed) creature. She has a fairly high tolerance for the antics of the Mermaid, until jealousy escalates between them. Although Pixies are generally calm, they can be provoked into a hair-pulling scenario by a raucous Mermaid. Pixies can also befriend one another, but they are most likely to surround themselves with male creatures, as friends, partners, and admirers.

The athletic, fun-loving Pixie enjoys all kinds of sports activities on a date. Take her horseback riding and then share a picnic in a meadow or go surfing and dine on the beach. When things get romantic, she is playful and enthusiastic, if somewhat less passionate and rather more predictable than a Wood Nymph. Many male creatures seek Pixies out for their low-maintenance personalities, but some, like the Centaur, Urban Elf, Tree Elf, and Hob, may not find them challenging enough for a long-term relationship. A Pixie's own tastes run toward the Woodsman; he is as attractive and friendly as she is. She also likes Tree Elves and Mermen, although she may not settle down with either of these types. She might consider the Tree Elf too "out there" or extreme, and the Merman's energy can be a bit heavy and slow for her. Although she is relaxed, she has a bouncy quality that needs to be met by her partner.

Many female types dream of being a Pixie, but it's not as fun as it seems. Although she is well liked wherever she goes, partly due to her confidence and ability to fit in to many different situations, she can be wrongly judged as having less depth of character than she really has. The Pixie may feel burdened by the projections placed upon her, as well as by the jealousy she stirs in some types. Mermaids handle this easily and tend to expand rather than contract in the face of it. The Pixie can become somewhat withdrawn, and her beaming smile may be less visible. When this happens, she needs to retreat to beautiful surroundings with her most trusted friends. She'll resurface soon enough, ready to take on the world and perhaps having gained some depth.

My children's preschool teacher was a Pixie. When I first met her I judged her as being somewhat superficial and without much compassion because she was a bit abrupt with me. She was trying to train a group of parents to work at the cooperative preschool and this postpartum Wood Nymph burst into tears when my daughter bumped her head. But I calmed down and the Pixie warmed up. She is actually one of the most empathetic creatures I know. However, she can appear detached because she stays focused on keeping herself fully intact while helping others. This is a trait that Dryads could learn from Pixies. The Pixie friend I now love is a great mom and champion of children. She is very attractive but never vain, friendly but self-contained, and a natural leader who never imposes her will but usually achieves her goal with her personable nature and intelligent perceptions.

MERMAID: THE DIVA

You can generally spot a Mermaid by her flowing, or meticulously cut, usually blonde hair, curvy or just very graceful body, and impeccably made-up face. She is always dressed glamorously, with an eye for designer labels, bright colors, and bling. She works out and eats carefully to stay in shape and get attention for her great body but not because she enjoys exercise as much as some of the other types do. She will definitely consider plastic surgery without wincing. Her voice is often low and compelling. Male creatures want her and she knows it. She tends to involve herself in the performing arts, like acting or singing, and is comfortable going by her first name, as she feels she is unique enough not to require a surname. Although she may appear somewhat superficial, she is quite intelligent and not without real depth.

A Mermaid is not always the easiest creature. She loves her freedom and takes a long time to settle down. She will challenge you at every turn and sometimes cause great pain. Mermaids can appear very sociable, saying hello to everyone they see, but they have a harsh edge, a judgmental nature, and a sharp tongue that keeps them somewhat removed. Beneath this exterior, however, Mermaids have warm, nurturing, maternal hearts, and if you gently but firmly tell one that she has offended you, she will own up to it and try to make amends as best she can.

Here's a story about a Mermaid friend:

I was confessing that I felt insecure about my appearance.

My Mermaid said, "Do you feel insecure about your face *and* your body, or just your face or just your body?"

I started to answer when she interrupted, "Because your *body* is perfect."

I was very offended and told her so. She tried to make it better, putting her tail deeper into her mouth with every word ("I meant your face is okay but your body is really great, oh, you know what I mean . . .").

Finally she blurted out, "If you were a guy I'd want to fuck you, OK?"

I started laughing and couldn't be angry anymore.

TESS: THE GENTLE MOTHER

Pretty. Friendly. Maternal. Loyal. Kindhearted. Compassionate. Intuitive. Generous. These are all traits of the Tess, a term derived from the word Giantess. Unfortunately, the sensitive, giving Tess may not know how to put herself first frequently enough. This selflessness is one of her love-liest qualities but can also be problematic for her and lead to depression. Some Tesses might do well to take a lesson from a Mermaid and behave in a more self-serving way now and then.

Tesses are naturally quite shy, so they are not easy to meet. They tend to be homebodies and enjoy the comforts of a lovely, feminine environment. They are not as extensive collectors as Giants but share their male counterpart's aesthetic. You will always find attractive cur-tains on their windows and soft pillows on their couch. Their cup-boards are well stocked, and they are often quite good, healthy cooks, unless they are feeling depressed, in which case they might tend to eat unhealthy, store-bought food to comfort themselves.

Most Tesses work at jobs of service in public institutions, where they feel safe and protected and are also able to give of themselves. Many are in health care or education. They are devoted to their work and do well at it but are not usually particularly ambitious or driven.

The young Tess, when faced with conflicts growing up, probably withdrew into herself and closely observed what was going on around her. She likely became an avid reader as a way to escape and to learn more about others in a safe way. Her introverted behavior has made her extremely intuitive, and she can readily resolve conflicts be-tween her friends and knows how to appease. These traits also help to make her an excellent mother. She has a calm, comforting effect on other creatures, especially little ones, unless she is feeling agitated herself, in which case she can be quite sharp.

The Tess may have difficulty in romantic relationships, as her feel-ings are so easily wounded. Like the Nymph, she has a deep longing for a profound partnership, but unlike the Nymph, she will not readily make this need known. It would serve her to confidently, if subtly, embrace her desires rather than feel ashamed of them. The right part-ner will come along if she is patient and learns to care for herself first.

Tesses tend to have excellent discipline, consistency, and stability with children and romantic relationships, although they may struggle with these issues when it comes to caring for themselves. This is partly due to the Tess's basically stoic nature and her tendency to put others first.

Wood Nymphs are another type who often make loving mothers, but they aren't always the most disciplined or consistent parents. On the other hand, they can be very disciplined and consistent in their creative endeavors and in taking care of themselves, since they know they might otherwise fall apart. These two types can definitely learn from each other in more than one way.

My children's other preschool teacher was a lovely Tess who always knew how to solve conflicts among the kids with her wisdom and soft-spoken manner. We became friends and I told her about the Satyr I was dating. One day she inquired how things were going with him.

"Has he talked about commitment?" she asked me.

I told her that he had said, "The only time is now," whenever I mentioned the future. (This is classic Satyr lingo, but I didn't have this system at the time.) The Tess replied, "The only time is now to break your heart." I was upset with her but, of course, she was right. Tesses are very astute about other creatures. Because they are often quiet observers, they learn to recognize signs that others might miss (not that this sign was hard to miss, but I was a love-struck Nymph). The trouble with this keen sense of observation is that it can inhibit the already shy and reticent Tess from taking risks in her life. I encouraged her to try online dating and she encouraged me to be more circumspect about whom I dated. She was also a wonderful resource for tips on how to raise my young ones.

BANSHEE: THE WARRIOR

The Banshee is a more rarified and intense version of the Wood Nymph. She is characterized by her extremely passionate nature and is subject to outbursts of anger and even violence. Banshees who channel their rage into creative expression (usually singing) can be geniuses in their field. They often have very strong opinions about everything from world politics and ecology to personal interactions. They are not afraid of the word *feminist*. A Banshee will tend to downplay her femininity with an androgynous style, but her potent sexuality will often be apparent in spite of this. It is not uncommon to see a Banshee with a shaved head, piercings, and tattoos as expressions of her rebellious nature. She is usually not particularly materialistic and lives a simple lifestyle but can also be brutally ambitious in her chosen field. As mentioned, many Banshees gravitate to singing, but they can also be involved in the visual and healing arts. A number of them are trained as counselors, but they are not always entirely suited to this work. Even though they are intuitive, intelligent, and compassionate, they are not known to be disciplined with their emotions and can overreact in delicate situations. Still, their ambitious natures usually garner them a good deal of success with whatever they do. They are driven not by desire for wealth but the desire for true love and the chance to change the world with their idealistic principles.

Although most Banshees care tremendously about the state of the planet, and they may become real activists, their lives generally revolve around their connections with a few close companions and the creative work they do to express their feelings about these often tumultuous relationships. Banshees make surprisingly good mothers because of their passionate devotion to their offspring. They are also uninhibited and creative lovers, much like Nymphs. However, Nymphs are usually appeased and calmed by sexual encounters, whereas a Banshee can become more agitated from them. One of the best things about sex with a Banshee, however, is that she will make her needs known freely. Mermaids are also good at this, but most types, including the generally uninhibited Nymph, have trouble with it, thereby lessening their sexual enjoyment and ultimately the enjoyment of their partners. If you're a more inhibited type, you might want to take a lesson from a Banshee and ask for what you want.

Banshees can be fiercely loyal to their friends and will stand up for you without flinching, but they are also very selective about their friends and don't get close to a lot of other creatures. They are usually soft-spoken unless they are screaming out song lyrics, and in spite of their aggressive style there is often a delicacy to their appearance. Because of this, they may catch you off guard when you get on their wrong side. A Banshee might not attack directly; she will write a vicious song about you or post something scathing on her blog. She may also "act in," hurting herself rather than you. Banshees must be watched closely when they are at this stage, so that they do not do severe damage to themselves. Luckily, they have their creative expression to help them through. If you know a Banshee in distress, help her find the tools, inspiration, and support to channel her upset into her art. This can be helpful for anyone, but especially for Wood Nymphs and Banshees. Because of their similarities, these two types often make good companions for each other.

I adore my Banshee. We always joke that we should find male creatures with each other's exact astrological chart (or perhaps mythological types) because we are so well suited to each other. We dance wildly together and write poetry to each other. We love to go to cafés and share apple tartin à la mode, creature watch, talk about our art, and laugh about our tormented relationships with male creatures.

She's always very protective of me and threatens to call up my badly behaved dates or colleagues and scold them. While we are both artists, her work is bolder, bloodier, and extremely powerful. She has worked as a stripper and can sing like Alanis Morissette. She has tattoos and wants more.

Sometimes I wish I wasn't such a heterosexual creature by nature. But it's good to have a Banshee on your side in any capacity.

HOBBY: SAVVY ON HEELS

The Hobby is very similar to her male counterpart, the Hob, although she is not as extroverted or overtly aggressive. This practical, somewhat conservative type doesn't always stand out at first, because she may not seek attention in the same way other types do, but she has many wonderful qualities that are worth exploring.

The Hobby is the quintessential career creature, on the way up the proverbial ladder of success. She did well in school and earns a decent salary. She considers herself a bit of a classic. She is not the most sensually inclined of the types but thoroughly enjoys a good bar of chocolate and the right jazz CD.

A Hobby likes to talk on the phone for hours. She uses this pastime to relieve tension, so she is very dependent on her cell. She doesn't really enjoy exercise, but she probably makes herself work out and chats to get her through.

It may not seem on the surface as if the Hobby is that interested in romance, but her reserved, practical approach to life hides a more sensitive soul. Although she is not as passionate as the Urban Elf (another type who keeps a good deal of her inner life private), the Hobby can be more tender than she appears. Her feelings are easily wounded and she may lash out when this happens—often taking her friends and partners by surprise. Because she seems quite confident on the surface, her companions don't feel as if they have to walk on eggshells around her. In fact, they do need to be sensitive. Although a Hobby won't admit that she has been wounded, she will react and retaliate with a witty, sharp comment or by using a more subtle condescending tone. Because she is so intelligent and perceptive, her zingers can really hurt and achieve the desired effect of putting offending parties in their place. Sometimes the Hobby attacks without provocation; the best way to handle this is to speak softly and firmly, politely drawing a clear boundary. She will usually back down at this, as she really is not born to fight. A Hobby would rather spend her energy getting to work on her next project, then kick back in her peaceful home environment that she has outfitted with all the latest technology. Like Urban Elf females, Hobbies are very self-sufficient and not only pay the bills but also fix things around the house with ease. They rarely present themselves as tom-creatures like Brownies do; they like to maintain an impression of understated femininity.

When it comes to relationships, a Hobby secretly longs for someone who will be highly attuned to her feelings, but it may take her a while to find this in a partner. The reason for this is that she may adopt an aggressive attitude with someone she likes, thereby scaring away the more sensitive creatures she actually desires. Another reason that it may take a Hobby a while to meet her proper match is that she tends to be unconsciously drawn to judgmental types like Hobs, who won't soothe her ruffled feathers. Many Hobbies, like Hobs, had problematic relationships with their mothers when they were growing up, and this friction often affects their adult partnerships.

Unlike the Hob, however, the Hobby will not complain overtly about her past. She maintains a "grin and bear it" attitude. Actually, it might serve her to express her feelings more. She believes that other creatures would take advantage of her vulnerability if they discovered it when, in fact, revealing herself carefully, and in the right company, could actually make her stronger and deepen her relationships.

My friendship with a Hobby was successful for many years until we finally outgrew each other. As I became a more assertive Wood Nymph and she gained power in her field we ran into conflicts. She would call herself a genius and refer to me as "missy." When I finally stood up to her, she bristled and we had a falling out. However, I am still indebted to this intelligent, quite brilliant Hobby for her help over the years.

BROWNIE:
THE CREATURE NEXT DOOR

These tom-creatures are athletically inclined like Pixies but to a greater degree. They work out at the gym consistently with an emphasis on gaining physical strength. This always cheers them up if they are feeling down. They are also often good at competitive sports. In keeping with these athletic interests, their style is casual, comfortable, sporty, and practical. They know about fat content and how to count calories but enjoy splurging on a rich dessert. Brownies are less intellectual than female Urban Elves, but they are naturally bright and have quick minds. However, they are somewhat naïve about the subtle dynamics in relationships. This is one way in which they differ from the savvy Hobby, although these two understated types can sometimes be confused for one another. The smile on the Brownie and her infectious laugh always give her away. Her grin lights up a party when she enters, completely transforming her face and the energy in the room.

Brownies are usually less at ease with other female types but easily befriend males, especially Fauns and Woodsmen. They have been known to fall prey to Satyrs, but less often than Nymphs do. Brownies like sex sometimes, but it isn't as radically important to them as it is to Wood Nymphs. For the Brownie, friendship and play always come first. She may have tricky relationships with her parents, especially her father, but will rarely admit to this. She likes to appear confident and comfortable in the world. Sometimes her exaggerated smile is actually a cover for a darker underlying view. Although sensitive herself, she may say insensitive things to others, usually when she is faced with an upsetting or emotionally charged situation that feels too difficult to handle. In this way she is very much like the Hobby.

When either of these types lash out, remind yourself that despite their tough stance, they're sensitive underneath it all and won't react well to outright criticism. Be patient with an aggressive Brownie and you'll soon see that dreamy smile again.

I know a Brownie who really did turn the world on with her smile. We were friends for years and had a lot of fun together, going on runs, going dancing, seeing live bands. I admired her many talents in the arts and sports. She seemed to know everyone wherever we went, and male creatures were very attracted to her athletic body and shiny, blunt-cut hair, stirring up my Wood Nymph jealousy. Perhaps I stirred up something in her as well because tension built between us over the years. When I confessed that a Faun I was dating didn't want to have sex with me, she grinned and said cheerily, "I wish I had that problem! My Satyr won't leave me alone!" Whenever she saw my boyfriends, she would give them a big squeeze and tell them how cute they were. She even did this one night when she knew I was emotionally dealing with a miscarriage. I told her that these things upset me and admitted to my insecurities, asking her if she might have some of her own that were adding to the problem. She became very defensive and accused me of having serious problems that she did not have. Maybe she was right. We lost touch until one day I ran into her with her Satyr, who was on his way to becoming a Woodsman, and their baby. We greeted each other politely but never revived the friendship. Still, I was impressed with the sweet family she had created and reminded of all the things I admired about her—feistiness, creativity, and the charm to transform a wayward Satyr into a happy family man.

VAMP: THE MYSTERY CREATURE

On the surface, the Vamp, or female Vampire, may not have much in common with the Mermaid, but look closer and you'll see that these two female types are not so dissimilar. Both Vamps and Mermaids like to draw attention to themselves. They are both attracted to the performing arts. They place a lot of emphasis on their physical appearance and know how to seduce with their sexuality. You can recognize both of them almost immediately, as they tend to identify themselves by their type. While Mermaids generally have long, fair hair and like to wear attractive, shimmering colors, Vamps usually have flowing, dark locks and dress in sexy black clothes. Some Vamps prefer a sweeping, romantic style with a revealing bodice, and others like severe, tight garments, but there is always some provocative, unconventional element involved. Mermaids tend to have voluptuous bodies that they proudly draw attention to, while Vamps are generally more self-conscious, at least when they are not performing. In spite of these differences, the emphasis on the importance of image and the need to show it off at all times is the same for both of these types.

Mermaids are generally more confident than Vamps, who, like Vampires, use their personas as a way to hide from the world rather than to showcase themselves as Mermaids do. Mermaids are also more high maintenance, while Vamps tend to take their upset feelings out on themselves rather than on others. They may exhibit some self-destructive behavior, especially in their youth. Vamps get depressed fairly easily; when this happens they often retire to their beds to try to sleep it off.

The Mermaid and the Vamp could be described as the dark and light of the same type, both challenging but always interesting mates.

To get to know a Vamp intimately, you need to prove that you understand her and care about her interests, which often include philosophy, spirituality, and the arts. Try talking to her about classic literary and possibly Gothic writers. Ask her about bands like Death Cab for Cutie, Muse, Joy Division, New Order, the Cure, and Echo and the Bunnymen. Pay attention to what she is wearing and discuss her philosophies about life. If you don't know a band or book she mentions, don't try to pretend that you do; just ask her. Vamps are very irritated by poseurs, and would much rather you be honest with them than pretend to be cool.

Even if you are patient and conscientious, it isn't always easy to get close to these enigmatic types. They like to keep a cloak of secrets wrapped closely around them.

On a date, a Vamp likes to be taken somewhere unusual. She'll appreciate watching a film screening in a cemetery. She also likes old movie theaters, decrepit carousels, abandoned grand hotels, and underground nightclubs where, after a few drinks, she will lose her inhibitions and dance seductively to live bands. Appeal to her sense of mystery and dark romance and you may win her over.

In bed, the Vamp tends to be less experimental and adventurous than her persona might lead you to believe. In fact, the cultivation of this elaborate, somewhat ostentatious persona can be a cover for a rather shy, sensitive creature. She is at heart often a traditionalist and likes to be romanced and treated with patience. But as with most creatures, if you are kind and respectful she may eventually open up and embark on sensual adventures with you.

I befriended a Vamp online and found her much more sensitive and gentle than her glamorous photos suggested. She was passionately creative as a painter and poet and devoted almost as much creative energy to her physical appearance. Her eye makeup and lipstick always looked perfect, and she wore her dark hair long and straight. She presented herself quite erotically in her pictures but was often surprised when male creatures responded sexually to her, as she was rather naïve about the impression she made. It turned out she really had no idea how attractive she was and often put herself down while at the same time being very supportive of her female friends. This lovely Vamp infatuated me and I feel more connected to her kind through our acquaintance. Isn't that always the case?

I also now have a dear Vamp friend who is studying to be a therapist. She has worked as a hostess at a trendy restaurant and as a band stylist, dresses like a rock 'n' roll chick, and has one of the most sensitive hearts of anyone I know.

WEREGIRL: THE CHARMER

The charming Weregirl can seduce male and female types alike with her sexy ways and friendly, extroverted personality. She will flatter you and offer to help you out. However, she always wants something in return so be aware.

A Weregirl likes to pose as the girl next door, easygoing and not particularly unique or threatening, although she usually favors a rock 'n' roll style with layered hair, band T-shirts, skinny jeans, and Chuck Taylors. She can be mistaken for a simple Pixie type—athletic, extroverted, and friendly. She might also be tagged as a Brownie, with her pretty smile and athletic body. But a Weregirl is usually much more edgy, intelligent, and even calculating than she might appear. Only her rather wild, somewhat unfocused eyes give her away. She has an almost compulsive desire to acquire what is not hers, a trait also not uncommon in the ambitious Hob and Hobby. Werewolves, the Weregirl's male counterpart, are usually not this way. They are content with their lives and don't want to draw too much attention to themselves for fear of having something disrupted. But Weregirls are always seeking to better their lives, environments, and physical appearance, sometimes to a fault. They will go about this more aggressively than the Hobby, who tends to pursue her goals with subtle drive.

Weregirls are usually very outgoing and will get to know you quickly. They will introduce themselves, ask your name, and shake your hand. They will always be sure to use your name when speaking to you, both as a way to put you more at ease and to stay in control of the situation. Although the Weregirl appears quite friendly, she will often speak behind your back and stir up trouble among her friends and acquaintances. However, she is so intelligent, fascinating, and charming that some types will put up with her worst qualities in order to enjoy her best ones. She can be a wild date, up for any kind of adventure, and she knows how to cast quite a spell in bed when she's feeling inspired or wants something from you.

The most troubling aspect of the Weregirl is how she behaves when under the influence of drugs or alcohol. She is prone to substance abuse and can easily get carried away. Like the Werewolf, when she is inebriated her whole personality changes radically. But whereas the Werewolf often becomes more irritable and somewhat paranoid, the Weregirl will become extremely extroverted and completely uninhibited, thus getting herself into some difficult or even dangerous situations.

The best way for a Weregirl to avoid the allure of excessive substances is to pursue physical activity. It always soothes her, and her natural strength and competitive nature make her a gifted athlete.

It's easy to meet these outgoing types. She'll usually capture the attention of all the males in the room, though, so you'll have to stand out to attract her interest. But that doesn't mean being the loudest, flashiest creature in the room. She is drawn to strong, silent types who accept her as she is and don't try to change her. Even though her own style can be understated, it's always thought out and she can be a bit judgmental about the appearance of others, so you'll want to be well groomed and stylishly dressed to win her. A Werewolf in his "darker" state does not appeal to her because he reminds her of her own dark nature. She is wildly drawn to Satyrs and also likes Tree Elves, but can be almost abusive to Giants, Urban Elves, and Hobs. Weregirls have built a lot of their identity around their sexuality and know how to use it to get what they want. This means she is a fun partner to play with, but also a somewhat risky one, so be circumspect before getting involved with her.

My experience with a Weregirl was very upsetting. She befriended me with compliments and favors and I soon fell under her spell. The only clue that I had cause for alarm was when she once revealed that she had spent her youth sleeping with a different creature every night and was known for stealing her friends' boyfriends. She said this proudly and laughed it off.

The Weregirl began to spend time with me and with that pesky Satyr boyfriend I was seeing. One day she and I were hanging out at my home with our kids when he called to say he was coming over. She immediately went home and returned a short time later in a dress and wearing lipstick. She was carrying a plate of meat and potatoes.

"I had to change because I had butt sweat!" she announced.

He ignored her and went to sit outside by himself. She grabbed the plate of food and pranced out to give it to him.

"I know you Satyrs like to eat meat, and Nymphs don't ever serve it!" she exclaimed.

He thanked her.

She sat beside him, touching his arms and shoulders, giggling and flattering him. Satyrs eat this kind of attention up. Nymphs don't serve much meat, it's true, but they don't respond well when someone tries to hit on their love interest either.

The next day I told Were gently that I didn't like how she had behaved. She got very upset and insisted that I was being overreactive and insecure. Her response was so harsh that I began to slowly back away from her over the next few months.

I made the mistake of confiding in the Satyr about what had happened. Satyrs have no patience with female jealousy, although they often intentionally provoke it, and he was only irritated by my response.

The day after we broke up, the Satyr revealed to the Weregirl that I had "some issues" with her and was avoiding her because I was jealous of her. She wrote me a vicious e-mail calling me every name imaginable. Soon after that she invited me to a party, sending me a chipper message that expressed her interest in remaining friends with me, but I couldn't overlook the cruel e-mail. Nymphs in particular have difficulty with forgiveness when such strong language has been used. I am now more cautious around this potentially dangerous forest type. However, for those who like excitement and magnetism in a partner, the Weregirl is a satisfying choice.

Male Combinations

If you still don't see yourself, you may be a combination type. All types can combine in various ways, but certain combinations are more common than others.

The **TREEHORSE** (Tree Elf/Centaur) is a creative healer. He's the doctor who paints, sculpts, or does ceramics in his spare time. He may wear his hair a little long and has trouble accepting the fact that he is aging since he feels like a twenty-year-old. He will chat about his previous career as a rock musician while examining you, and he may flirt harmlessly. This creature uses his creativity to enhance his profession, distracting and pleasing his patients with the artistic part of his personality so that the healer can best do his work.

Another male combination type is the **URBAN HORSE**, a blend of the Urban Elf and Centaur. This rather eccentric creature is extraordinarily intelligent, gifted, and capable, although slightly awkward socially and quite absentminded. He has a fierce creative drive hidden beneath a somewhat reserved exterior. Like the Urban Elf, he usually sports small glasses that may sit slightly askew on his face. His hair is often long, and he generally has a bit of stubble on his chin, or possibly a few razor nicks. He is a rather shy and can appear aloof. However, he is more passionate than the common Urban. His work is usually in science, education, or the arts. Imagine the classic absentminded professor, genius type like Albert Einstein, and you have the Urban Horse.

The **WOOD CENTAUR** is a Centaur who, usually at around the age of fifty, decides that he would be better off with a little stable love in his life than painting alone in his studio to the end of his days. He will then find a nice female creature to settle down with. This isn't that hard for him, as his creativity and steady (if somewhat slow-arriving) commitment to family can be very attractive to many female creatures. Wood Nymphs do especially well with this type, if they can catch him at the right time of life. The Wood Centaur may choose a somewhat younger mate, since his artistic nature needs to be nurtured and pampered, especially as he ages. In exchange he will provide stability and stimulation for his partner. He may lose himself in his work on a regular basis but will usually emerge from it refreshed.

The **WATERHORSE** is a Centaur and Merman combined. While the typical Merman is focused on anything and everything to do with water and nature, the Waterhorse divides his time between nature worship and the arts. He is happiest when he can combine these two passions. He may paint, sculpt, or build. His work is always imposing and takes physical strength to produce. He may incorporate natural materials like driftwood, shells, and sand into his pieces. He is attractive to many creatures, but his interest in his work and the natural world border on the obsessive. This is due to the fact that both Centaurs and Mermans have this obsessive bent to their personalities. The Waterhorse can be especially hard to reach when he is caught up in one of his reveries.

TREE GOATS are not that different from a typical Tree Elf, but they are more extreme in their sexual pursuits, thus the Goat moniker derived from the goatlike Satyr. They combine the Tree Elf's fascination with nature and healing with the Satyr's sensuality. A positive aspect of this type is that they are very up front about their interest in sexuality so you know where you stand with them. They are comfortable with the term *polyamory* while a Satyr avoids this term at all costs, rightly fearing it would lessen his chances of conquest with many a female creature. Tree Goats can be found at contact dance classes, improvising touchy moves with a succession of partners, and at yoga retreats, music festivals, and New Age seminars. Some become sexual gurus or even cult leaders. As long as you know what you are in for, this type can open up whole new worlds of sexual healing through the tantra.

TREE HOBS are an unusual type, as the laid-back Tree Elf and ambitious Hob are so different from each other to begin with. A Tree Hob should try to integrate the two parts of his nature. He will be successful combining his healing and business skills in his work. Many conventional doctors are this type. They have the Tree Elves' instinct to help others and the Hobs' practicality and business sense. This type will work hard all week in the office, earning a good deal of money, and then spend the weekend frolicking happily on a golf course, where the green reminds him of his partially elfin nature.

The **URBAN GOAT** (Urban Elf/Satyr) is a tricky sort. He may appear harmless and mild mannered at first but can use this cover to mercilessly seduce his prey. You will find this type in office jobs; however, the entire raison d'être of the Urban Goat is Satyr-sex, and success in business is only a means to that end. This type can be even wilier than the Satyr because he is very cerebral as well as instinctual and knows how to manipulate others with his brain *and* his charisma. Urban Goats are not for the faint of heart, but if you can recognize them for what they are and not get too attached, there is a lot of pleasure to be had with this type. They have all the lust of the Satyr mixed with the precision and skill of the Urban Elf and can provide hours of fun between the sheets.

URBAN HOBS tend to combine some of the most challenging aspects of both the Urban Elf and the Hob. They are very cerebral and may sacrifice emotional warmth and compassion for knowledge and financial success. Sometimes they come from painful childhoods in which they felt belittled and are constantly trying to prove themselves. Some psychiatrists and clinical scientists like biologists fall under this category. They can have somewhat exploitative aspects to their personalities. A positive aspect of the Urban Hob is that his ambitious, analytical mind can sometimes make great discoveries that benefit creaturekind, even if his daily encounters may sometimes be a bit chilly.

A **WATERWOOD** is a Merman and Woodsman combined. The Merman's connection to nature grounds him and often prepares him to turn his attention to family life after a time, especially as he realizes he is getting older and won't be totally self-sufficient forever. If he does focus on family, he will probably behave in a manner similar to that of the Woodsman, bringing home the fish, building the fire, and reading tales of the sea to the children. He can be a devoted partner and father, but he will never give up his love for the outdoors. If his mate can share him with Mother Nature, they will be able to forge a happy, peaceful life together.

The **WOODFAUN** is a Faun who has given up some of the freedoms of his youth to be a husband and father. He is usually kind and playful, if a bit lazy in these roles. He does best partnered with an even-tempered type like a Pixie or the high-energy Brownie, who can handle some of the extra chores he may neglect. His charming, youthful soul can connect easily with his children, although he may be less successful at handling some of the responsibilities inherent in parenting.

WOOD HOBS are the businesscreatures who finally realize that life is passing them by and they haven't spent enough time with their family. This may happen due to a wake-up call related to physical illness, as high-powered Hobs are sometimes prone to stress-related maladies. But when the Wood Hob turns his attention to his home life he is a delightful father. You can find him every weekend in the backyard grilling hot dogs or playing basketball with his kids.

HOB GOATS get away with a little less than proper Satyrs or Urban Goats because their Hobness makes them less subtle about their lustful ways. Their prey will recognize them and often be able to avoid their advances, at least for a time. However, the advantage the Hob Goat has over the Satyr and even the Urban Goat is his persistence. He will be as determined to conquer the female creature of his choice as the regular Hob is to succeed on the job. Whereas the Satyr uses his grace and charm to do this, the Hob Goat will use his financial success and aggressive personality to lure his creatures. He may leave them quickly for the next, but he does know how to wine, dine, and romance any creature who captures his fancy.

A **VAMPIRE GOAT** is a mix of Vampire and Satyr. They may look like your typical pale, elegantly dressed Vampire, but while the Vampire has developed his persona for complex reasons (that may include sexual reasons), the Vampire Goat is interested in this façade for one purpose only—it's a great way to get Vamp chicks! This type is problematic for any Vamp or Vamp combo type because she may not recognize him at first, mistaking him for a regular Vampire. The Vamp likes consuming, passionate, monogamous love relationships and will not put up with the Vampire Goat's promiscuity for long. If he loves her enough he may be able to evolve out of his Goat self.

As mentioned, creatures can evolve from one type to another. Centaurs and Tree Elves are likely to become partial Woodsman, especially after becoming fathers, but this rarely happens with Fauns or Satyrs. An Urban Elf with a lot of therapy, yoga, and a vegetarian diet can become a Tree Elf. Hobs may change into Urban Elves if they pursue therapy, yoga, and meditation. Giants tend to stay true to their original natures and rarely change. What is most important to note about the concept of the evolving male type is that one mustn't expect this to happen. In other words, as hard as it is, especially for a powerful female with a strong imagination (Wood Nymphs and Dryads in particular), keep your eyes open and don't fall in love with potential. You may want to learn to appreciate each type for who they are and not try to change them at all!

URBAN FAIRIES are a subtle blend of their namesakes. They are the most style conscious of Urban Elf females. Although they favor the Urban's glasses, sweaters, and skirts, they choose only the best quality of all these things. They will almost always name Miuccia Prada as their favorite designer because she combines high fashion with a highly intelligent aesthetic. The Urban Fairy tends to work in the fashion industry, where she can utilize her creative talents and sharp intellect.

Fairy/Mermaids, or **FAIRMAIDS**, are outgoing in the world but homebodies at heart. They can strut around in high heels all week and then spend the weekend at home making pretty curtains and staring at shoes on the Internet. They are maternal and enjoy the role of mother as long as they can maintain a sense of glamour in their daily life. They appear tough, but their feelings are easily wounded.

NIGHT FAIRIES are Vamps and Fairies combined. They are a rather unusual type, as the Fairy's soft sensibility generally clashes with the Vamp's darker image. However, when these two types come together it makes for a fascinating creature. She is extremely feminine and creative, rather moody, and always alluring.

MER-SHEES (also known as **SIRENS**) are Banshees and Mermaids and rival the Night Mermaid in terms of their personal power. The Mer-shee is constantly changing her image; one day she may have dreadlocks to her waist and the next she may be bald. Everything she does is for dramatic effect. She is often a performer, combining her forceful, almost masculine presence and voice with a feminine glamour. She can lure her audience to behave in strange and unpredictable ways; imagine a Siren sitting on the rocks combing out her hair and calling sailors to their death with her exquisite voice and you have a sense of the power of the Mer-shee.

NIGHTMERS are Mermaids and Vamps. Although the Vamp's name might give you the impression that she is someone who takes advantage of others, this is not the case. She is usually too shy and unsure of herself to manipulate others very well. However, when combined with the dynamic Mermaid, the insatiable part of the Vamp's nature emerges more readily, and she may be willing to exploit almost anyone in her life who can feed her in some way. This unusual combination is powerful; she can change the world if she wants to, but she can also be extremely self-serving.

HOB GOATS get away with a little less than proper Satyrs or Urban Goats because their Hobness makes them less subtle about their lustful ways. Their prey will recognize them and often be able to avoid their advances, at least for a time. However, the advantage the Hob Goat has over the Satyr and even the Urban Goat is his persistence. He will be as determined to conquer the female creature of his choice as the regular Hob is to succeed on the job. Whereas the Satyr uses his grace and charm to do this, the Hob Goat will use his financial success and aggressive personality to lure his creatures. He may leave them quickly for the next, but he does know how to wine, dine, and romance any creature who captures his fancy.

A **VAMPIRE GOAT** is a mix of Vampire and Satyr. They may look like your typical pale, elegantly dressed Vampire, but while the Vampire has developed his persona for complex reasons (that may include sexual reasons), the Vampire Goat is interested in this façade for one purpose only—it's a great way to get Vamp chicks! This type is problematic for any Vamp or Vamp combo type because she may not recognize him at first, mistaking him for a regular Vampire. The Vamp likes consuming, passionate, monogamous love relationships and will not put up with the Vampire Goat's promiscuity for long. If he loves her enough he may be able to evolve out of his Goat self.

As mentioned, creatures can evolve from one type to another. Centaurs and Tree Elves are likely to become partial Woodsman, especially after becoming fathers, but this rarely happens with Fauns or Satyrs. An Urban Elf with a lot of therapy, yoga, and a vegetarian diet can become a Tree Elf. Hobs may change into Urban Elves if they pursue therapy, yoga, and meditation. Giants tend to stay true to their original natures and rarely change. What is most important to note about the concept of the evolving male type is that one mustn't expect this to happen. In other words, as hard as it is, especially for a powerful female with a strong imagination (Wood Nymphs and Dryads in particular), keep your eyes open and don't fall in love with potential. You may want to learn to appreciate each type for who they are and not try to change them at all!

Famous Types

This is a list of well-known celebrities and their type—a fun way to help figure out types in your own life. As you'll note, some categories are more full than others, since certain types are more likely to show up in the public eye. Can you add to this list?

CENTAURS
CELEBRITY:
Clive Owen, Johnny Depp, Daniel Day-Lewis, Sean Penn
CLASSIC:
Humphrey Bogart, Orson Welles

TREE ELVES
CELEBRITY:
Paul Simon, Jackson Browne, James Taylor, David Gray

WOODTREE (WOODSMAN AND TREE ELF)
CLASSIC:
Paul Newman

URBAN ELVES (MALE)
CELEBRITY:
Daniel Radcliffe (Harry Potter), Moby, James Spader
CLASSIC:
Fred Astaire

GARDEN ELVES
CELEBRITY:
Jude Law, Hugh Grant, Joe Jonas, Zac Efron
CLASSIC:
Rudolph Valentino

WOODSMEN

CELEBRITY:

Robert Redford, Brad Pitt, Denzel Washington, Jake Gyllenhaal, Matt Damon

CLASSIC:

Jimmy Stewart, Henry Fonda, Gene Kelly

MERMEN

CELEBRITY:

Jeff Bridges, Gary Busey, Kurt Russell, Patrick Swayze, Nick Nolte, Matthew McConaughey

CLASSIC:

Johnny Weissmuller, Lloyd Bridges

WATERHORSE (CENTAUR AND MERMAN)

CELEBRITY:

Keanu Reeves

GIANTS

CELEBRITY:

Gerard Depardieu, Luciano Pavarotti, Bill Murray, Francis Ford Coppola, Steve Martin

CLASSIC:

Spencer Tracy, Walter Matthau

SATYRS

CELEBRITY:

Warren Beatty, Kobe Bryant, Trent Reznor, Anthony Kiedis, Colin Farrell, Russell Crowe

CLASSIC:

Cary Grant

HOBS

CELEBRITY:
Woody Allen, David Sedaris

CLASSIC:
Groucho Marx

FAUNS

CELEBRITY:
Tom Cruise, Brendan Fraser

CLASSIC:
Clark Gable

VAMPIRES

CELEBRITY:
David Bowie, Tim Burton, Christopher Walken, Nicolas Cage, Marilyn Manson, Perry Farrell

CLASSIC:
Edgar Allan Poe, Salvador Dalí, Vincent Price, Jack Palance

WEREWOLVES

CELEBRITY:
Kurt Cobain, Heath Ledger, Bob Dylan, Robert Downey Jr., David Duchovny

CLASSIC:
James Dean

WOOD NYMPHS

CELEBRITY:
Rachel Weisz, Penélope Cruz, Maggie Gyllenhaal, Sofia Coppola

CLASSIC:
Sophia Loren

DRYADS
CELEBRITY:
Sarah McLachlan, Jewel
CLASSIC:
Judy Collins, Joan Baez, Carole King

WOODTREE (WOOD NYMPH AND DRYAD)
CLASSIC:
Joni Mitchell

URBAN ELVES (FEMALE)
CELEBRITY:
Jodie Foster, Lisa Loeb, Tina Fey
CLASSIC:
Emily Dickinson

FAIRIES
CELEBRITY:
Kate Moss, Renée Zellweger, Cate Blanchett, Nicole Kidman, Michelle Williams
CLASSIC:
Audrey Hepburn, Veronica Lake

FAIRNYMPH (WOOD NYMPH AND FAIRY)
CELEBRITY:
Sarah Jessica Parker

PIXIES

CELEBRITY:

Jennifer Aniston, Cameron Diaz, Reese Witherspoon, Kate Hudson, Goldie Hawn

CLASSIC:

Doris Day

MERMAIDS

CELEBRITY:

Beyoncé, Madonna, Sharon Stone, Jennifer Lopez, Scarlett Johansson, Kim Cattrall, Queen Latifah, Pamela Anderson, Tyra Banks

CLASSIC:

Elizabeth Taylor, Mae West, Jayne Mansfield, Rita Hayworth

MER-TREE (MERMAID AND DRYAD)

CELEBRITY:

Oprah Winfrey

FAIRMAID (FAIRY AND MERMAID)

CELEBRITY:

Marilyn Monroe

TESSES

CELEBRITY:

Kate Winslet, Julianne Moore

CLASSIC:

Ingrid Bergman

MERTESS (MERMAID AND TESS)

CLASSIC:

Meryl Streep

BANSHEES

CLASSIC:
Sinead O'Connor, Alanis Morissette, Tori Amos, Ani DiFranco
CLASSIC: Sylvia Plath

MER-SHEES (MERMAID AND BANSHEE)

CELEBRITY: Angelina Jolie, Tina Turner

HOBBIES

CELEBRITY: Diane Keaton, Laura Linney, Helen Hunt
CLASSIC: Katharine Hepburn

BROWNIES

CELEBRITY: Julia Roberts, Sally Field, Mary Tyler Moore,
Anne Hathaway, Geena Davis

WOOD BROWNIE (WOOD NYMPH AND BROWNIE)

CLASSIC: Judy Garland

VAMPS

CELEBRITY: Helena Bonham Carter, Cher, Dita Von Teese, Christina
Ricci, Elvira, Lisa Marie Presley
CLASSIC: Carolyn Jones (Morticia Addams), Maila Nurmi (Vampira)

WEREGIRLS

CELEBRITY: Winona Ryder, Lindsay Lohan, Britney Spears
CLASSIC: Greta Garbo, Anne Sexton

WERE-MAID (WEREGIRL AND MERMAID)

CELEBRITY: Courtney Love

Types in Literature

The forest folk types are endlessly portrayed in popular culture. Ancient myths and fairy tales as well as more contemporary literature are full of references to them.

It is interesting to note that certain types dominate the protagonist role in most stories. Why is this? It seems to me that this has to do with the fact that historically our culture has valued traditionally strong male types (like Woodsmen, Centaurs, and even Satyrs) and apparently passive female types (Pixies, Fairies, Tesses) over more introverted males like Urban Elves and Hobs and assertive females like Mermaids and Banshees. (Of course, all types can have assertive and passive characteristics, although one part usually dominates.) I tried to find stories that feature each type and hope to come across more from a new generation of writers who showcase the less visible types in their work. Why not a Faun hero and a Hobby heroine?

BEAUTY AND THE BEAST is an example of a story of a sweet but brave Fairy and a Giant in his home full of magical collectibles, such as a talking mirror, and his enchanted rose garden.

SNOW WHITE AND THE SEVEN DWARVES is about a nurturing Dryad and seven Woodsmen who care for her.

LITTLE RED RIDING HOOD is a perfect expression of the dynamic between a Satyr and a feisty, if somewhat naïve, Brownie.

CINDERELLA is a classic Pixie–Garden Elf tale. The dynamic Pixie is really the focus of the story, and the more passive though loving Garden Elf is especially interested in her shoes.

The myth of **CUPID AND PSYCHE** is an example of an overly passionate Wood Nymph in love with a skittish, mother-dominated Faun.

ARACHNE in Greek mythology is an industrious and competitive Hobby weaver who is punished by the goddess Athena (another Hobby?) for her boasting and her skill, and changed into a spider.

ODYSSEUS is a Merman who leaves his loyal Tess wife, Penelope, to go on a journey in which he meets the beautiful, controlling Mermaid-type Calypso, who tries to imprison him on her island, and the Banshee-type Circe, who bewitches him.

NODENS, the Celtic god of health, is an example of a Tree Elf.

HAMLET is a classic Werewolf torn between two parts of his nature.

JANE EYRE is a smart yet plain Urban Elf, and Edward Rochester is a moody, passionate Centaur.

Gothic novels feature many Vampires and Vamps, most notably the Count and Lucy in Bram Stoker's **DRACULA**.

MADAME BOVARY is a tragic Weregirl tale in which the main character indulges her passions in adulterous affairs and finally swallows arsenic and dies. I hope someone writes a nice, positive Weregirl one of these days!

In "**THE LOVE SONG OF J. ALFRED PRUFROCK**," a frustrated middle-aged Hob tries to express his thoughts and feelings in a rather neurotic yet extremely poetic and beautiful way.

The protagonist of J. D. Salinger's **CATCHER IN THE RYE** is a sensitive Urban Elf becoming cynical in the city.

Mythological Matches

HOW THE TYPES RELATE
TO EACH OTHER

Female-Male Matches

Now that you are familiar with the types, you may want to examine how they pair up. What challenges will a Fairy find with a Giant? What are the joys in a relationship between a Wood Nymph and a Satyr? How can an Urban Elf and a Vamp learn to get along?

I have paired all the male and female types to find the easiest and most difficult combinations and will suggest ways to make things work for even the most challenging pairs. Because in the forest of life, love can conquer all if both creatures are willing to work at it.

 WOOD NYMPH (Female) **✝ CENTAUR** (Male)

As soon as she sees a true Centaur, a Wood Nymph may hear this sound in her head, or even utter it aloud: "uh-oh." She knows this is the creature she has been imagining as her partner since she was a little woodland creature. She also knows that she is going to be especially vulnerable and could get hurt. But this won't stop her. The Nymph's high libido and expansive heart will not let her rest until she gets closer to this alluring beast. He's less intuitive about relationships and will ignore the "uh-oh" if he hears it at all. He has never spent much time ruminating about what his future partner will be like, although he is often physically attracted to a wide range of creatures. He may be too occupied with his current project to notice her at first. But a Centaur will like the Wood Nymph's creativity and will especially admire her sexual energy. However, it is possible for his fragile artist's ego to be threatened if she has achieved more success with her art than he has. This will make him turn away from her and pursue his work even more adamantly, causing her to feel rejected. He won't be fully present in bed or out, and this can drive a Wood Nymph wild with frustration! If she is patient with him, and if he can achieve some level of success to match hers, they are the perfect couple, filled with sexy, creative passion. Their fights might be frightening to witness because Nymphs have trouble controlling their tempers, and Centaurs, although usually calm, are fearsome when they are finally provoked enough to unleash their anger. As a compensation for this, their make-up lovemaking can be some of the hottest in the forest!

 ## WOOD NYMPH *(Female)* + TREE ELF *(Male)*

This couple is easily drawn together, and they seem familiar to each other right away. The Wood Nymph will love the Tree Elf's warmth and outgoing personality as well as his healing abilities. He will want to nurture her and help her develop her self-esteem. They'll probably end their first meeting with a big, warm hug, and when things get intimate they will enjoy playful sex with lots of eye contact and communication. Their mutual interest in the arts and psychology will make for long conversations outdoors over healthy picnics. The challenges come when the Wood Nymph realizes that her Tree Elf's warmth and nurturing qualities aren't reserved for her alone. He wants and needs to connect to a lot of creatures, even if he's only sexually involved with one. This can be hard for the jealous Wood Nymph, and she may act out. The Tree Elf will try to work with her on this because he likes to heal his relationships, but after a while he can get impatient. If she admits to her own part in the conflict and he is willing to hang in there a little longer they can forge a passionate and long-lasting bond.

WOOD NYMPH *(Female)* **+ URBAN ELF** *(Male)*

The Wood Nymph will be attracted to the Urban Elf's intellect and elegance, and he will like her wild sexuality and emotional nature, as long as she doesn't try to get too close; then he will retreat into his shell or even lash out at her. If she goes slowly and doesn't pressure him, they can enjoy trips to museums, cafés, and bookstores, followed by exotic sex, although she may miss the eye contact and tender emotional exchanges she so cherishes. If these two decide to take it to the next level, the Wood Nymph will have to calm her temper and work on healing her insecurities, and the Urban Elf may need to open his heart.

WOOD NYMPH *(Female)* **+ GARDEN ELF** *(Male)*

A Wood Nymph will think she recognizes herself in the Garden Elf, who can fall passionately in love, has a lot of energy to create beautiful things, and gets his feelings hurt easily. They will become fast friends, and she'll put up with his sarcasm for a while because she loves how witty he is and because he knows how to have fun with her. But if he takes his edgy humor too far, she will turn her back on him harshly and he may not be able to redeem himself in her eyes. He in turn will be offended by her rejection. After a time apart they may miss each other enough to reinstate their relationship and take on the rest of the forest creatures together, searching in solidarity for like-minded creatures to populate their social circle.

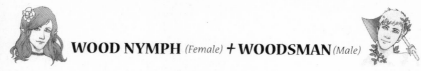

WOOD NYMPH *(Female)* + WOODSMAN *(Male)*

The Wood Nymph will avoid the Woodsman because she immediately assumes he is too physically attractive to notice her. She will also make judgments about his intellectual prowess and emotional depth as a way to defend herself against being rejected by him. A Woodsman might actually not notice the Wood Nymph since she becomes so shy and retiring around him. Even if he does notice her, his attention might be captured by a more confident creature. However, if the Wood Nymph takes a chance and unleashes her sexuality on the Woodsman, he may be impressed and want to get to know her better. She may find that he has more depth and warmth than he appears to have and she will become especially excited when she sees how he behaves with children—her heart will fill with dreams of settling down and starting a family. A Woodsman may be seeking a slightly more stable mate for this endeavor, but if he is swept up in the Wood Nymph's sensual spell, he may decide to take a chance on her. She makes a surprisingly good mother when she is feeling supported, and he a surprisingly loyal mate; they will always enjoy their private time at the end of a long day.

WOOD NYMPH *(Female)* + MERMAN *(Male)*

A Wood Nymph needs a lot of attention, but in certain relationships she can sacrifice this need. She has an innate understanding of how the creative process can become an obsession for the Centaur. She can also understand the Satyr's focus on sex, as they share this interest. But she is less likely to understand other obsessions, so when the Merman reveals his love affair with nature, the Wood Nymph may be confused.

She will try to stay engaged with him because she likes his physical strength, friendly personality, and somewhat spiritual leanings. He usually finds her wildness attractive, not unlike his true love, the ocean. But ultimately these two may struggle to find things to talk about, and sex between them can become frustrating. The Wood Nymph will tire of trying to keep the Merman's attention, and he will get distracted when her curves remind him of a ski slope or her movements of a wave.

 ## WOOD NYMPH *(Female)* + GIANT *(Male)*

Giants are less obsessive about Wood Nymphs than they are about Fairies, but they can become easily enamored with these creatures as well. A Giant will wine and dine the Wood Nymph and want to give her gifts. He will listen attentively to what she has to say and not be intimidated by her emotions or creativity. He will be reticent about approaching her sexually and wait for her cue. If the Wood Nymph is attracted to the Giant, she may initiate a sexual encounter, confident that she will not be rejected. But he may snap at her defensively as they become intimate, especially if he is at all insecure about his own sexuality. After this occurs, she may pull away until one of them reaches out again. If they end up together this cycle can repeat for years. The good news is the loyal Giant and expressive Wood Nymph will usually stick together once they make this commitment, however challenging it may be.

 ## WOOD NYMPH *(Female)* + SATYR *(Male)*

On the surface, these two look like the perfect pair. They are both passionate and share a palpable physical chemistry. In the bedroom, the more adventurous and generous Wood Nymph may get a little tired of the Satyr's tried-and-true methods, ones that mostly satisfy him (sometimes at her expense), but she's sure to be excited by his lusty ferocity and confidence, especially if she's just recently been in a relationship with an Urban Elf or Faun!

What will most likely come between them is the Wood Nymph's emotional needs—the Satyr just can't be there for her in the ways that she wants, and she may become more and more demanding. Unless he is able to evolve, either through therapy or age or true love, the Satyr will shy away from this pressure and use it as an excuse to move on to his next conquest, leaving the highly emotional Wood Nymph temporarily heartbroken.

Not to worry; her high libido and warm heart will help her heal and find a more suitable partner. She must always remember not to take things too personally when it comes to relationships, especially with a Satyr.

 WOOD NYMPH (Female) **+ HOB** (Male)

The Wood Nymph will be initially put off by what she considers to be a judgmental attitude from the Hob. She'll think he is criticizing her at every turn, and he may be. He finds her usually messy hair and emotional rawness a bit disconcerting and will not understand her unconventional thought processes, spiritual leanings, or style. In turn, she will be bewildered by his combative attitude. If they can realize that his aggression and her emotional exposure (or overexposure) are defenses that cover the same insecurities, they may be able to let down their walls and begin to develop a relationship based on sharp intellect and high energy.

WOOD NYMPH *(Female)* + FAUN *(Male)*

These two will probably like each other right away. Fauns admire creatures who express their passion and know how to channel it. Wood Nymphs will feel safe with the Faun's gentle nature. He doesn't stare at other creatures when he is with her. He is sensitive to her feelings and always polite. He won't be threatened by her strength. She likes how cute he looks. She might not be conscious of it, but having an attractive date makes her feel better about herself. There will be a sweet, flirtatious attraction between them. If they start to date, they will have pleasant encounters, enjoying similar films, music, and social activities with friends. Their kisses will be full of passion and tenderness. However, the Wood Nymph may feel something lacking as the relationship progresses and the Faun does not meet her needs. She may feel rejected by his passivity and start to look for things to criticize about him. She will notice for the first time that he might not be quite as ambitious as she is, and his lack of material success may start to bother her. This in turn will cause him to become defensive and shut down. Still, a solid camaraderie is at the core of this relationship; even if these two cannot fulfill each other romantically, they have a good chance of staying friends.

WOOD NYMPH *(Female)* + VAMPIRE *(Male)*

The Wood Nymph may distrust the Vampire's cool demeanor. He may be put off by her effusive personality and lack of attention to details about her appearance and lifestyle. Her taste in music, art, film, and fashion may overlap with his, but her range of interests is usually much broader. He can be a bit of a snob, only associating with creatures who have almost the exact same aesthetic as he does. It is unlikely that they can get past these stylistic differences, but if they do they may find they relate to each other at least as creative friends or sources of inspiration.

 ## WOOD NYMPH *(Female)* + WEREWOLF *(Male)*

Wood Nymphs may mistake a Werewolf for a Centaur or Faun and become quickly enamored with him. He seems like the all-around creature she's been looking for—friendly, creative, intelligent, and attractive, with some sense of style. But there is something vaguely disturbing about him that she can't define. When he overindulges around her, this elusive something becomes clear. If his dark side doesn't show itself right away and she has already become attached to him, she may stick around and try to help him overcome his addiction, but if his shadow is revealed early on, she may be scared off at the first sign of it. His erratic behavior reminds her of her own emotional ups and downs, and it scares her. He may have been initially attracted to her because he assumes that she is open-minded and nonjudgmental and can understand his quixotic nature, so he'll be surprised and upset by how reactive she can get when she feels insulted or threatened in any way. It's usually best for these two to work on their issues separately before they attempt to come together.

 ## DRYAD *(Female)* + CENTAUR *(Male)*

Dryads and Centaurs make a good match. She's probably as devoted to her work as he is to his, so there won't be tension between them if one or the other disappears into a project for a few days. They'll come back together with lots of ideas to share and renewed passion for each other. He brings out her more ambitious side and she brings out his tenderness. They could easily start a family together, although most of the work of raising children will probably fall on her. She'll be able to handle this and still maintain her connection to her work, as Dryads have a great deal of energy for multitasking. They'll rarely fight because they both have a rather high emotional intelligence quotient, and the Dryad is an expert at communicating her feelings in a non-threatening way. If she does feel upset he'll know how to calm her with his quiet but strong reassurance.

My parents were this type of couple. My father, a painter, flourished with the encouragement and devotion of my Dryad mother. My mother grew more secure in herself as she became his muse. She didn't feel the need to compete with him creatively because she felt her contributions were expressed in the art itself. She was also very content to turn her energies to mothering me and my Woodsman brother while my father focused on his creative work and in turn encouraged me in mine. Centaurs often father Wood Nymphs or Banshees!

DRYAD *(Female)* ✛ TREE ELF *(Male)*

This match is quite common and usually successful. These two healer types are likely to meet through work, volunteering, or recreational activities and have much in common. They both want to make the world a better place, and this passion fuels their romantic relationship. They will be so absorbed in sharing the same activities (hiking, yoga, massage, natural foods, etc.) and working toward a common goal that there won't be time for many problems to arise between them. Their sexual connection usually has a spiritual component. Sometimes the Dryad can be inhibited in bed, due to her extremely sensitive nature, but the Tree Elf can help free her of some of her fears. If they have a disagreement they know how to talk it out respectfully. The only real challenge for these two is the Tree Elf's extroverted manner with other females. The Dryad is much less overtly flirtatious than he is. She's quite tolerant, but after a certain point she may feel threatened and he'll have to tone down his full-body hugs and touchy dance moves a bit to appease her.

My favorite Dryad/Tree Elf combination is a couple in their sixties who have been together for twenty years. He does transformational massage and she provides healing energy work, using her master's in education, her studies with the Maori, and her natural psychic abilities. They are always able to work out any issues between them, using highly developed communication skills. It's a joy to be around them, and they provide hope for Dryads and Tree Elves everywhere.

 ## DRYAD *(Female)* **+ URBAN ELF** *(Male)*

Urban Elves tend to be very attracted to Dryads. She represents a part of himself that he was in touch with as a young Elf, possibly a Tree Elf in the making. As he got older he may have lost this link to the natural world and spirituality and he'll try to rediscover it through her. They can have a very powerful connection during this phase of the relationship. The Dryad will usually feel safe with the Urban and begin to explore her sexuality with him. However, he may eventually feel threatened by her ability to open up emotionally and by her request that he do the same. If he can manage this they can have a lovely, long-lasting relationship, but if not, trouble will escalate and they may not be able to transcend it.

One Urban Elf I dated was still married to a Dryad. Although she had left him years before, they remained close friends and the intensity of their relationship continued to pose an emotional threat to the new significant others in their lives. He was particularly proud of the fact that she taught yoga and meditated, never wore makeup, and saw him for who he really was, and he compared me to her more than once. Any female creature who involves herself with an Urban Elf should check to make sure this tenacious type is really done with his previous relationship before getting in too deep. Conversely, any female creature who was previously involved with a smitten Urban can probably expect him to show up again some day if things didn't end too badly.

 DRYAD (Female) **+ GARDEN ELF** (Male)

I know a Dryad/Garden Elf couple who are deeply in love. The Garden Elf feels immediately calmed and comforted by the Dryad's steady presence. He really can't get enough of her. While he can be critical of certain types, he's particularly sensitive to her and will rarely utter a harsh word to or about her. She adores him, too. They share a love of flowers, nature, and beauty. Their romance is sweet and tender, soothing to both of them.

 DRYAD (Female) **+ WOODSMAN** (Male)

One reason why forest folk come together is so we can grow through the challenges the relationship presents. The Dryad and the Woodsman won't particularly challenge each other. Although the Woodsman can be content with this, the Dryad is usually seeking ways to further her personal growth. She may not be attracted to the Woodsman for this reason. If she doesn't pursue him, he won't necessarily notice her, and they'll move along the forest path separately. If they do decide to come together, and I know more than one couple that have, they'll have a very pleasant relationship and may choose to raise a family. The Dryad will then probably focus on her offspring as a way to fulfill her needs for growth.

DRYAD *(Female)* **✝ MERMAN** *(Male)*

This is an easy and quite common match. The Dryad's love of nature meshes well with the Merman's fixation. She's a grounding force for him and he inspires her. The Merman can teach the Dryad that all the truth she seeks lies in the natural world that she loves so much, and she can help him to understand the emotional ocean that lies within him. They are both free spirits, but the Dryad is sometimes a bit cautious and the Merman can help her expand her horizons. I know one such couple who consciously chose not to have children but to travel around the world instead, sharing many wonders.

DRYAD *(Female)* **✝ GIANT** *(Male)*

Dryads and Giants get along quite well. The Dryad has the feminine charms of the Fairy and the creative energy of the Wood Nymph, but she's less demanding and restless than either of these two types. The Giant will admire her and she'll deeply appreciate his kindness, his refined aesthetic, and his nurturing manner. They'll be able to cultivate a tender relationship, if not the most fiery one. The challenges arise if the Giant relies excessively on the Dryad to heal his childhood wounds. He needs to take responsibility for this himself (perhaps with a Dryad therapist and not a mate). His Dryad love will want to help him, and she won't resent his needs, but the relationship can become unbalanced if she neglects her own needs for his. I advise my Dryad friend in this situation to always remember to care for herself first. She tells me that I'm just as much a Dryad as she is in the way I sometimes problematically put others' needs before my own.

One librarian Giant and massage therapist Dryad I know seem to blissfully dance through life together, enjoying the pleasures of nature, books, and experimental healing techniques.

DRYAD *(Female)* + SATYR *(Male)*

As self-aware as the Dryad is, she can still fall prey to the Satyr's advances, especially if he is disguised as a Tree Elf. The Tree Goat is a dangerous match for the Dryad. He'll use all his Tree Elf skills of healing and compassion to lure her into bed and then reveal his Goatish self as he leaves her for the next female creature. This can devastate the sensitive Dryad. While some types can handle a Satyr, the Dryad should probably avoid him altogether.

DRYAD *(Female)* + HOB *(Male)*

The somewhat critical Hob may alienate the sensitive Dryad when they first meet. He won't understand why she's avoiding him because he often doesn't realize when he's hurt someone's feelings. As far as he can see, she's a lovely creature whom he wants to know better. If the Dryad can gently explain her feelings to the Hob, he may be able to soften his approach with her and they can begin to get closer. Still, they are quite different and it might not last.

In one case I've observed, the Hob's abrupt sexual advances seemed insensitive to his Dryad. He is more materialistic and doesn't understand why the Dryad can't seem to handle her money in a more practical way or dress more conventionally. She wants him to reveal his vulnerabilities, not realizing that he has constructed his whole life around keeping them hidden, or only expressing them through humor and sarcasm. They'll have to do a lot of negotiating (and consulting a mythological dating guide!) to make this work.

DRYAD *(Female)* + FAUN *(Male)*

While these two are likely to befriend each other, things may not heat up into romance. The Faun will be attracted to the Dryad's healing qualities and she'll value his compassionate listening skills and gentle manner. He might not fully get all of her interests in crystals or astrology but he won't dismiss them outright. She might think he spends too much time at the gym but she understands that it is his way of avoiding more destructive addictions. Neither of these types are particularly aggressive sexually, though they both enjoy affectionate touch. They may end up doing a lot of hugging and not much else. They'll probably stay good friends, no matter what.

I know a Faun and Dryad, still spry in their seventies, who had a romance when they were young and met again in their fifties. They dated for a while but she decided to call it off when a Werewolf came into the picture. Things didn't work with the problematic Werewolf and the Faun was still there waiting, twenty years later. They are now close friends, although she can be a bit impatient with him. (I think she's a bit of a Wood Nymph.)

DRYAD *(Female)* + VAMPIRE *(Male)*

Vampires and Dryad's won't have much opportunity to meet. They live in such different worlds and usually surround themselves with other likeminded folk. It might be as simple as the fact that Vampires are part of a night world and Dryads love the light. If their paths cross at dawn or twilight they might not know what to say to each other. Still, a true Dryad is able to see beyond the surface of things and it is possible for her to "create the space" (her language) for them to come together.

DRYAD *(Female)* + WEREWOLF *(Male)*

The Werewolf who feels at the top of his game probably won't seek out a Dryad type. He'll be nonchalantly pursuing Mermaids or Vamps, perhaps a Fairy. But when the Werewolf falls apart, he'll be able to fully appreciate the charms of the healing Dryad creature. He'll need her to help him through his darkest times, and she'll be a wonderful companion. She's attracted to the hurt part of him and can see it right away, while other types might miss it. Their romance will be fueled by the dynamic of the wounded one and the healer. While this might not work as well with the Giant, the apparently stoic Werewolf can rely heavily on the Dryad for a long period of time without damaging the essence of their relationship. He may have a setback now and then and she'll still be there for him. As long as he is serious about healing himself, they can work well together for a long time and both benefit from the experience. In the most effective example of this pairing that I know, the Dryad, who came from an abusive background, nurtures her Werewolf while he makes her feel protected from the dark shadows of her past.

URBAN ELF *(Female)* + CENTAUR *(Male)*

In the case of one Urban Elf/Centaur couple I know, he sees her true sensual nature and can coax it out more efficiently than almost anyone. She thinks he's a genius and will encourage him ardently.

Unfortunately, the Centaur is sometimes too scattered and frankly too sloppy for her taste. She gets irritated quite often. She doesn't like the messes he makes, how he tends to show up late, and how he doesn't call her when he says he will. He doesn't like being scolded and becomes even more troublesome in response. If pushed too far, either of them may seek solace from a more understanding creature and their relationship will suffer.

URBAN ELF *(Female)* + TREE ELF *(Male)*

The Tree Elf can be a refreshing, playful partner for the more introverted, studious female Urban. He may take her to explore nature and awaken her hidden passions under an oak beside a babbling brook. She in turn can help the sometimes distracted Tree with the task at hand. Her discernment and organizational skills are as beneficial to him as his spontaneity is to her.

The Urban Elf could become impatient with the Tree Elf's exuberance, and he may sometimes long for a more adventurous partner, but all in all this is a good match. I know a librarian Urban and her deejay Tree husband who have made it work.

URBAN ELF *(Female)* + URBAN ELF *(Male)*

These two Elves are so similar that they seem like the perfect match, but this isn't always the case. They often work for the same techy/artsy companies and frequent the same places on their off hours. They enjoy the same books, music, and general aesthetic. They even look alike. However, they may be put off by the cool demeanor they see in each other; it reminds them of a part of themselves they don't always want to be ruled by. Many Urbans are initially attracted to overtly warmer types like Centaurs or Dryads. But if one or both of them are willing to take the risk and open their hearts, they can form a powerful and long-lasting bond.

One of the happiest couples I know are Urban Elves. She had been through a series of failed relationships with Satyrs when she met this Urban. They are practically the same person—thin, with matching glasses, smart minds, and quiet but hysterically funny personalities. He's in computers; she's a writer. They move to different cities depending on his work, but their homes are always located near museums, bookstores, and good coffeehouses. They aren't going to have kids, but they are wonderful parents to their beloved cats.

URBAN ELF *(Female)* **+ GARDEN ELF** *(Male)*

These two make a great team. His innate sense of style and her traditional education and technological skills combine to help them achieve success. However, he can get impatient with her detachment. He may seem cool himself, but he actually likes touchy-feely creatures best; they soothe him. After a while, she may become offended by his sharp tongue. It's worth it for them to invest time in working these issues out because their talents are so complementary. One Garden Elf I know inspires his Urban and found the perfect glasses to suit her face, while she grounds him and helped transform his dreamy scheme (an eyewear boutique!) into a reality.

URBAN ELF *(Female)* **+ WOODSMAN** *(Male)*

This is an unusual combination. The Urban Elf will secretly crush on the Woodsman but she won't expect him to be interested in her. She also may judge him as being superficial or not particularly intelligent.

He's so used to being approached by female creatures that he's a bit lazy about doing the work himself. Her shyness and his laziness may make it difficult for them to know each other. If she shows him her sexier side (and it's there!) he may pay attention. If they settle down together—I know one example—he'll make such a good partner and father that she will forget she was ever concerned about the fact that he hadn't read Chekhov.

URBAN ELF *(Female)* + MERMAN *(Male)*

The Urban Elf is unlikely to meet the Merman for the simple reason that one loves the city and one loves the wild. If they happen to come together, perhaps on a vacation, he can introduce her to the gifts of the ocean and the hillsides, and she can impress him with her sophistication and intelligence. However, it is difficult to imagine these two sustaining a relationship beyond a temporary experimental fling.

URBAN ELF *(Female)* + GIANT *(Male)*

Fast friends! You'll find these two at library or comic book conventions, running from exhibit to exhibit and chatting about everything they see. Although they are both fairly introverted, they bring out the more extroverted qualities in each other. They are the serious types most likely to crack each other up. If romance develops it may be lukewarm, as the Giant generally relies on the sexual advances of his partner to provide the heat. The Urban Elf has the same tendency, so they may reach a sexual stalemate. However, their bond of friendship is so strong that it might not matter.

At book conventions (publishing again!) I see a certain well-known librarian Giant gallivanting around with at least one or two

Urban Elves on his arm. They laugh at all his jokes and admire his mane of red hair. They can deconstruct any novel together and share CDs of the latest art-rock bands.

URBAN ELF *(Female)* + SATYR *(Male)*

The female Urban Elf may not seem particularly susceptible to the Satyr, but she is actually one of his most vulnerable types of prey. She'll be attracted to his wildness because she tends to keep this part of her nature private and often needs to look outside of herself to find its expression. He will sense her hidden sensuality and feel challenged to bring it out. He will have librarian fantasies about her, imagining her taking off her glasses, unbuttoning her prim blouse, and letting down her hair. She'll have rock star fantasies about him, imagining him sweeping her off her feet on his motorcycle en route to his next gig. In reality, these two will gain things from each other and meet many challenges. He'll learn things about literature and music—knowledge he'll use to seduce the next creature if he moves on. She'll learn how to loosen up in bed and feel more free in her body in general. The Urban Elf isn't an overtly jealous type, but her feelings will be hurt by the Satyr's lustful wandering eye, and she'll turn a cold shoulder to him. He may accuse her of being prudish or chilly. If they break up it will probably be swift and silent because both share a tendency to avoid confrontation at all costs.

I know one Urban Elf in publishing (a favored field for them) who lived a double life. In the day she was always conservatively dressed, hardworking, and serious. At night she went to clubs with her Satyr boyfriend, stayed out late, and had wild sex with him. He was fun but never fully available and refused to sleep over or introduce her to his friends. Eventually she realized this wasn't the way she wanted to live her life. She is now happily engaged to a male Urban Elf graphic designer.

URBAN ELF *(Female)* **+ HOB** *(Male)*

Because both these types are drawn to urban areas, their paths are likely to cross, especially at work. The female Urban Elf is not very materialistic and may be turned off by the Hob's frequent references to money and power. He won't quite get her offbeat, understated style and quiet manner. They can work well together, however, as his ambition and her precision make for a good partnership. While engaged in this collaboration, some sparks may eventually fly between them and they can apply their considerable skills to a relationship. This happened for two of my friends, a young adult book author and her literary agent. Both are closet romantics, so a close, sweet bond developed once they felt secure with each other.

URBAN ELF *(Female)* **+ FAUN** *(Male)*

Two introverted types like this rarely engage with each other unless they are forced together. She may judge him as being a bit superficial, and he may think she lives too much in her head. If they are thrust together like one couple I know, they will find that they share a common sensitivity and intuition about others. He makes her feel and she makes him think. Their relationship might not become particularly romantic, however, as both are a bit reticent sexually (at least at first, in her case) and usually need encouragement from their partner.

URBAN ELF *(Female)* ✛ VAMPIRE *(Male)*

As an intelligent and intuitive observer, the Urban Elf likes to understand what makes this creature tick, but his ostentatious persona is a bit much for her. He enjoys the meticulous attention she pays to him but may not find her quite glamorous enough. If they do get intimate, their sexual relationship will be intense, with the Elf willingly playing the more subservient role, but she will never fully give herself to him as she might to another type. He'll be intrigued with this withheld aspect of her and it may keep him interested for a while. However, they'll both have to expand their horizons to make this challenging relationship last.

I know an Urban Elf screenwriter who is involved with a Vampire director, but she doesn't seem entirely at ease with the relationship and he tends to pay a little too much attention to his Vamp and Mermaid actresses for her taste.

URBAN ELF *(Female)* ✛ WEREWOLF *(Male)*

She'll fall for him right away. He's just rumpled-looking enough to seem vulnerable, unlike the male Urban Elf or Faun. She'll sense his dark side, but it won't be as obvious as the shadow that the Vampire wears on his sleeve. He has much more in common with her than the Merman or Hob does. He'll be able to engage in conversations on unusual topics like how to mix an authentic 1950s cocktail and what music topped the charts in 1946. He seems sweet and charming, and he'll appreciate her style and substance. The Urban Elf female isn't scared of darkness and she'll be able to take his Wolf side in stride most of the time, as long as he remains tasteful about it. He is prone to taking advantage of her giving nature, but if he's conscious he'll know how to avoid this.

The previous information was gleaned from a happily married Urban Elf/Werewolf couple I have the pleasure of knowing.

FAIRY *(Female)* + CENTAUR *(Male)*

Fairies may find the Centaur too distracted, moody, and unkempt for her taste. As impressed as she is by the work he does, she will want him to pay more attention to her and to his grooming standards. He may consider her a bit shallow. But if they give each other a chance, things may work out between them. He will find that she has much more emotional depth than is initially apparent. She will discover his ability for true intimacy, though it may be sporadic, and appreciate his passionate focus on her when they are making love.

Playwright Arthur Miller's marriage to Fairmaid Marilyn Monroe was a romantic, if ill-fated, example of this pairing. Monroe's sexuality and star qualities made her part Mermaid, but her sensitivity and depth are Fairy qualities. Miller, the intense, moody artist, was a Centaur.

One couple I know make this pairing succeed, staying fulfilled through their creative work (he's a writer and she's a visual artist and director), focusing on their children and finding time to explore their fantasies together.

FAIRY *(Female)* + TREE ELF *(Male)*

Fairies like Tree Elves as a rule, especially if they are combined with a more grounded type like a Hob. The Tree Elf will impress the Fairy with his expansive, generous persona, hugging her warmly and speaking openly about his feelings. She's less comfortable with these displays for herself but admires them in others. The Tree Elf will like the challenge the Fairy provides; he'll want to dissolve her defenses and win her heart. This dynamic will keep them interested for long enough to allow them to really get to know each other. They may share a lot of sexual chemistry, as the Tree Elf will rise to the occasion of freeing the Fairy from her inhibitions, and she will find his presence both relaxing and stimulating. They have common interests—Fairies are usually curious about the healing arts, and Tree Elves appreciate good style. She might get impatient with his lack of interest in material wealth, and he may roll his eyes at the number of shoes she's accumulated, but these are minor worries for them. The trouble can arise if the Tree Elf showers his affection too freely on others. Fairies don't appear to be jealous types, but they are much more sensitive than they seem and won't take well to this. The Tree Elf will be caught off guard by the Fairy's anger and it will take a lot of love for them to overcome this obstacle.

My Fairy friend and hairstylist got involved with an actor Tree Elf. On the night they met, he danced sensually with her, looked deep into her eyes, and told her she had a beautiful soul. He sang the lyrics of a romantic song to her as they danced. After they got together she reminded him of the first time they had met. He could not recall the evening, as he typically danced with everyone in this way. If she were a Wood Nymph or Banshee she would never have been able to forgive him, but as a Fairy she finally let it go and they are still (somewhat tentatively) together.

FAIRY *(Female)* **+ URBAN ELF** *(Male)*

Fairies tend to be rather cool at first, so they may not connect to the sometimes chilly Urban Elf. These two may admire each other from afar since both pay attention to their appearance and are well man-nered and graceful in public situations. Urban Elves know the value of beautiful objects, and the Fairy eye can be caught by the silver rings on his fingers, the good suede jacket he wears, and the pretty things he makes. In turn, he will want to catch her to study as a perfect specimen. When their curiosity overwhelms them at the same time they may step forward and meet. They can enjoy stimulating conver-sations and share similar interests. They are both sensitive and polite and will be careful not to hurt each other's feelings. Problems arise when the Urban Elf is cold to the Fairy. She will in turn pull away. This may create a stalemate that neither can break, and they probably don't have enough physical passion or true emotional intimacy to weather this storm. One of them will have to take a risk and open their guarded heart to make it work.

 FAIRY *(Female)* **+ GARDEN ELF** *(Male)*

These two have so much in common that they can't help but bond im-mediately. They can spend hours playing, shopping, and chatting to-gether, and when they collaborate creatively they make pure magic. A Fairy and Garden Elf can form a great design team, whether they are working in fashion, beauty, or interior décor. They always look good when they go out together because as meticulous as they are on their own, the presence of the other ups the ante for each. Both tend to be a bit competitive; this can push them to new levels, but it can also eventually drive them apart if they don't consciously protect the rela-tionship they have developed. Ultimately, they should be able to pre-serve the relationship; both tend to bring out the most nurturing and loyal aspects of each other.

The Fairy/Garden Elf pair I know met when they were both very young. She was a makeup artist and he an aspiring actor. It was love at first sight. After they had dated for a few weeks, she caught the flu and he brought her juices and herbal supplements. She knew from that moment that he was the Elf for her. Over time he became very successful in his career but never lost his tender, caring manner with her. They remain happily married and best friends through thick and thin.

FAIRY *(Female)* + WOODSMAN *(Male)*

Fairies are drawn to Woodsmen like birds to shiny objects. The Fairy's heightened aesthetic is as powerful as a Wood Nymph's libido and will cause her to overlook any fears she may have and pursue what she is attracted to. She'll also like the Woodsman's emotional and financial stability, which she values over other qualities, like mystery, intellect, or creativity. For his part, he'll be attracted to her feminine, sexy style and take-care-of-business energy. However, if the Woodsman is too vain or self-involved, the impatient Fairy will get fed up with him and scurry off to find a new creature friend. He may be left wondering what hit him before he picks himself up by his bootstraps, waiting for the next female creature to come along and pursue him.

A Fairy/Woodsman couple I know are devoted parents and keep their sex life alive, although he almost always has to initiate it. Their main arguments revolve around finances, since the Fairy is a bit of a spender. Overall, they have a very loving relationship and are likely to remain together forever.

FAIRY *(Female)* + MERMAN *(Male)*

She'll take one look at his flip-flops and wonder why she's wasting her time. However, the Merman is worth a shot. He'll be a loyal, loving mate for a Fairy if she can give up some of her superficial judgments and cosmopolitan aspirations, or at least settle for exploring that part of her nature on her own or with friends. He will give her the admiration she seeks and won't ask for much in return, except for her presence and the opportunity to follow his watery dreams.

A Fairy boutique owner and Merman swim coach I know didn't stay together romantically but are still the very best of friends and even share custody of their dog.

FAIRY *(Female)* + GIANT *(Male)*

A Giant loves Fairies and dreams of luring one to his abode. He knows how to impress her with beautiful things and flattery, but after a while a Fairy may get annoyed, even turned off, by his somewhat suffocating attentions.

I have a Fairmaid friend who was recovering from a divorce when a Giant found her. He was deeply smitten and wrote her admiring e-mails. He complimented her hair, her graceful walk, and even wrote admiringly about the brand of shirt she was wearing (although it was a Dolce & Gabbana when he thought it was a 7 For All Mankind, a label she—as part Mermaid—would never wear!). She was flattered, if a bit freaked out, at how much attention he paid to the smallest detail about her. She visited the Giant at his office and he gave her a tour, cracking bad jokes and showing her off to his colleagues. He invited her to his home, which was overflowing with tchotchkes. He cooked for her and served good wine. He admired her shoes. He admired her hair. He admired her Jil Sander shirt. He sweated profusely throughout. He talked about his surgery and physical ailments, which is common for Giants; they tend to be athletic when they're young, and then get lazy in middle age, which leads to various physical aches and pains. It was all too much, too soon! The Fairmaid tried to be polite, but she was finally unable to control herself any longer and escaped in a panic. When she got home, she e-mailed the Giant, politely telling him that things weren't working out. He didn't seem to get it and kept pursuing her. Even when her e-mails got somewhat harsh (she is part Mermaid, remember) he wouldn't give up and still tries, to this day, to win her over.

Even though there are many obstacles to this pairing, it can ultimately work if the Fairy learns patience (and can hold her tongue) and the Giant focuses on taking care of his own needs as much as hers. He must, above all, repress his natural tendency to pout when he doesn't get his own way (always a turn-off to a Fairy, especially one who is part Mermaid).

If a Fairy decides to give her heart to a Giant, she will be rewarded with the material gifts she loves, but, more important, with acceptance, emotional stability, and a lifetime of support in her creative endeavors. So Fairies, don't dismiss your Giant too quickly—he could become a stabilizing force for you and your sometimes flitty ways.

FAIRY *(Female)* + SATYR *(Male)*

Watch out, Fairy! The Satyr is going to look awfully good to you, especially if he is dressed to impress! You will be all right as long as you recognize the Satyr for what he is and act accordingly. If you can enjoy him casually for a while, go for it! Fairies tend to be able to do this better than Wood Nymphs or Dryads, but not as well as Mermaids. However, if a Fairy starts expecting the Satyr to settle down for the long run she will be in for a disappointment. Fairies don't give their hearts that easily, but when they do it is for keeps, so they have to be especially careful.

A Satyr can smell a Fairy a mile away and knows just how to lure one into his lair. She will respond to the chemistry he knows how to generate, almost single-handedly. His only disadvantage is that his highly sexual persona can look a little rough around the edges and overwhelm the refined Fairy, and he is not always skilled at cleaning himself up to meet her grooming standards. That is why a well-dressed Hob Goat is even more of a threat to a Fairy creature. The lesson here: Whenever you Fairies sense anything Goatish going on, keep your guard up. Satyrs will always benefit from their experiences with Fairies, who can unwittingly teach them more of what they need to know to seduce other females, and it is certainly possible for a Fairy to handle a Satyr, at least temporarily if not forever.

A Fairy I know met a Satyr on the Internet. Their first date was exceptionally romantic. The Satyr wooed the Fairy with sweet talk and delicious food and wine, so she was surprised when he didn't call her back. Two weeks later she sent him an e-mail thanking him for the date and making it clear she'd be open to seeing him again. He wrote back immediately and they went out that night. They drank sake and danced and sang in a private karaoke booth. They kissed and hugged and he ended up staying over.

She never heard from him again.

She eventually realized that she had been spared in the long run, but I do know of Satyrs who uncharacteristically yearn for the Fairies they've let get away.

FAIRY *(Female)* **+ HOB** *(Male)*

The Hob who watches his sharp tongue can lure a Fairy with his wealth and its manifestations. She'll like his suit, his car, his house and the dinners, beauty treatments, and presents he lavishes on her. He'll like having her on his arm, always looking pretty and pulled together, and he'll admire the way she gets things done with skill and grace. These two can have a very positive, productive relationship unless the more hidden parts of their natures surface. Fairies have a darker, passionate side that can outweigh their need for material comforts and they can be lured away by creatures who fulfill this part of them. Hobs have a competitive streak and a hidden vulnerability that can feel easily threatened. If this happens they may also stray, looking for someone who can give them consistent validation. The Fairy is not always able to do this, especially if she is caught up in her own concerns. If a rift occurs it will be difficult for these two somewhat stubborn creatures to heal their relationship.

A fictional Hob/Fairy combination that has worked so far, despite many challenges, is Carrie Bradshaw and Mr. Big from *Sex and the City*. However, his uncharacteristic (for a Hob) confidence makes him more of a Hob/Satyr combination. This is actually a good thing in the case of this relationship since, combined with Hob stability, it counteracts any desire he may have to leave her out of his own insecurities.

FAIRY *(Female)* + FAUN *(Male)*

A Fairy and a Faun will probably like each other well enough at first, based on grooming standards, style, and taste alone. But there won't be much sexual chemistry; both of them tend to keep their sexual energy toned down a bit and look to their partners to amp it up. The Fairy won't be particularly attracted to the Faun's lack of motivation; she is generally looking for a good provider, or at least someone to equally carry his weight financially. The Faun likes femininity but he is more attracted to strength, and the Fairy may seem too girly for his taste. If a Faun and a Fairy can get past these things, they can create a nice life together in which the emphasis is on caring for their children and nurturing and entertaining their friends rather than on the deep intimacy and passion between them.

I know a Fairy/Faun couple who are best friends as well as romantic partners. The Faun is usually calming the somewhat nervous Fairy down, reassuring her whenever she gets anxious. The Fairy pampers the Faun. They are both content with the lack of intense sexuality between them and enjoy the comfort they provide each other.

FAIRY *(Female)* + VAMPIRE *(Male)*

Fairies usually find Vampires a little too over the top for their tastes, but they may like their creativity and especially their glamour. Vampires tend to admire Fairies and want to catch one, at least for a brief encounter. A Fairy, in spite of her inner strength, can appear to be a damsel in distress, and this is a big turn-on for the Vampire. He imagines sweeping her away into the night as she cries out in protest. She in turn is somewhat attracted to danger, as long as it looks good. They can have fun together, but the Fairy has a mind of her own and may eventually get bored with a scenario in which she is always cast in the role of the weaker partner. When she asserts herself more, he may feel that she is judging his clothes, musical tastes, and late-night lifestyle and will defensively criticize her more conventional behavior, especially in the bedroom. If this happens they will drift apart. Some couples may transcend the novelty stage of their relationship and create something real, but it will usually involve a rather large transformation on the part of one or both of them. Because Vampires rarely change much over time, it is probably up to the Fairy to become part Vamp if this relationship is going to last.

FAIRY *(Female)* + WEREWOLF *(Male)*

Fairies have a good instinct about Werewolves (not their ideal match) and know how to avoid them. If the Werewolf woos the Fairy persistently and stays away from addictive substances, he may win her with his offbeat charm and creativity and the allure of his hipster lifestyle. But ultimately she wants more emotional and/or financial stability than he can probably provide, and she may flit away even before he's gotten himself into any real trouble. As with any combination, these two can make it work if they really want it. A Fairy may be so attractive to a Werewolf that he is willing to change for her, but she'll have to accept his quixotic nature and he'll have to stay clean and sober, making her his only "addiction."

The Werewolf and Fairy couple I know were on the verge of breaking up when he admitted to a sex addiction, but they were able to make it through this crisis together. The Fairy appreciated his ability to admit to his problem, and her dignified and cool but also warmly sexy persona made her well equipped to handle him.

PIXIE *(Female)* + CENTAUR *(Male)*

Centaurs can be competitive, and the easygoing Pixie rarely poses a threat. However, other issues could still cause problems. They'll enjoy each other in bed, but when they're not making love the Pixie will want to take her partner to the beach or on a bike ride, while the Centaur would usually rather finish his project. This alone may be enough to keep them from realizing a successful relationship, as it did for a Pixie actress and Centaur playwright I know. Still, neither type tends to hold grudges long so they have stayed friends in spite of their differences.

PIXIE *(Female)* + TREE ELF *(Male)*

A good match! Pixies might not seek out the secrets of the universe on their own time, but they'll be open to hearing what the Tree Elf has to share. He loves to teach and heal and give of himself in any way, especially to such an attractive, receptive, smiley audience. He'll take her on all kinds of adventures and she'll be up for it all. They can surf, hike, bike, camp, and travel together with ease. They'll have playful, passionate sex. The Tree Elf really brings out the Pixie's best qualities. She's not threatened by his occasionally wandering eye; she knows he's truly devoted to her. He may teach her compassion and encourage her to develop some latent Dryad-like qualities in herself. If they have children, they can build a joyful, thoughtful family life together.

The happy hiking Tree Elf friend I mentioned earlier told me that he always had dreams of Pixie babies, so he imagined he would probably end up with a Pixie. I took this as a sign that he wasn't interested in me romantically and crossed him off my crush list. Sure enough, he soon changed his Facebook status to "In a Relationship" and posted pictures of himself and a gorgeous, smiling Pixie frolicking on the beach and wine tasting on a pretty patio.

PIXIE *(Female)* + URBAN ELF *(Male)*

The Urban Elf will notice a Pixie across a room and find himself very attracted to her physically. He won't know exactly how to approach her and will assume she has a boyfriend or that she just won't be interested. If they are introduced, she may not see past the cool gaze behind his small glasses. She'll think he doesn't like her very much, and she's not used to that. She's not the type to take this as a challenge and will turn to someone who will return her warm smile. If the Urban can develop enough self-confidence, he may be able to break down the barrier between them. The problem is that although he may enjoy her company, she's not really what he's looking for anyway. He's more naturally drawn to Dryads or Urban Elf females. For her part, the Pixie probably needs a more easygoing partner. This isn't the most successful of pairs, but they'll probably feel that they've learned something from getting to know each other. One rather insecure Urban Elf I knew gained a great deal of confidence in himself as an attractive male from dating a Pixie. She in turn felt intellectually stimulated by the Elf.

 PIXIE *(Female)* **+ GARDEN ELF** *(Male)*

These two will be attracted to each other right away. However, she prefers a slightly more grounded type and he likes his female creatures with more of an edge. She would rather spend her time playing volleyball on the beach and he prefers the theater and a five-star restaurant. After the initial attraction wears off there might not be much to keep them together. Cameron Diaz and Justin Timberlake were an example. (Note the past tense.)

 PIXIE *(Female)* **+ WOODSMAN** *(Male)*

This happy, if somewhat conventional, couple represents what many creatures aspire to. They are attractive, friendly, and well adjusted. They can enjoy a pleasant family life together while maintaining their romantic attraction to each other. Neither tends to get restless unless a more aggressive type enters the picture. Woodsmen are especially susceptible to this (e.g., a very famous one who was married to a Pixie and then swept away by a gorgeous Mer-shee). Luckily, if this happens, the resilient, if temporarily brokenhearted, Pixie will not take long to find a new and perhaps even more stimulating mate.

One happy Pixie/Woodsman couple I know have been together for years. They started out as friends until the Pixie grew tired of being treated like a pal and gave him an ultimatum. Things quickly turned romantic and they have been together ever since, raising two sons and keeping up successful careers and many friendships.

PIXIE *(Female)* + MERMAN *(Male)*

This match is a no-brainer, as the happy-go-lucky Pixie and the laid-back Merman feel immediately at ease with each other. They can feel so comfortable, in fact, that there isn't enough sexual tension and they may decide to keep their relationship platonic (think Kate Hudson and Matthew McConaughey). Other Pixie/Merman couples can have a sexual connection that lasts into old age. Either way they'll get along famously with lots of twinkling smiles, warm hugs, and sweet chemistry. You can find these two on the beach getting bronzed in the sun and playing in the waves.

PIXIE *(Female)* + GIANT *(Male)*

While the Giant will appreciate the Pixie, she isn't always his type. He prefers a somewhat more complex creature with emotional issues that he hopes to soothe in some way. The Pixie is just so . . . happy all the time! She will be friendly to him but may not recognize his romantic interest in her, if it does develop. He's not really her type either. (Why does he care so much about those rocks he collects?) They can possibly develop a good working relationship but that's usually about the extent of it.

However, if the Giant has some Hob materialism and/or Woodsman domesticity, and if the Pixie can get over her somewhat superficial attraction to a certain physical type, this relationship can be great. Observe the characters of Charlotte and Harry in *Sex and the City*!

 ## PIXIE *(Female)* **+ SATYR** *(Male)*

Because the Pixie is fairly used to being approached by male creatures she'll be less susceptible to this one's lures than most. She may think he's cute and sexy and want to date him, but she's had enough experiences to know a player when she sees one. He'll be somewhat relieved that she recognizes his true character—it takes some of the onus off of him for once. If she gets involved with him, he will relax, knowing he won't leave her heartbroken. Even Satyrs have a conscience and they don't always want to break hearts; they're just doing what comes naturally to them. These two can have a lot of fun for a time, but it will rarely last. Even if the Satyr matures to the point of wanting to settle down, he will probably not pick a Pixie. He wants to grow old with a type who can understand the darker aspects of human nature, like the Brownie or the Fairy. On the other hand, the Pixie could be the perfect solution to his fickle ways and, like the Brownie, she'll allow him the freedom he needs. I have known Satyrs who have been left brokenhearted and pining away after happy Pixies.

PIXIE *(Female)* ✚ HOB *(Male)*

The Hob may annoy the Pixie at first because he is so aggressive. She probably has to deal with Hobs all the time in the world of business, so she may shy away from this type when it comes to romance. But a Hob confronted with a Pixie he likes won't give up easily. He rarely gives up easily on anything! As with the Mermaid, he'll pursue the Pixie until she gives in and goes out with him. He can be much more charming and romantic than he appears at first, and there's a good chance he'll be successful at winning her heart. A happy Hob is a pleasure to be around and he will soften and grow more generous from his relationship with the Pixie of his dreams. She'll help him learn to relax after a hard day and reap the benefits of his less stressed self.

PIXIE *(Female)* ✚ FAUN *(Male)*

Pixies and Fauns are both friendly and athletic, so they'll probably have an easy time meeting each other. They may even date based on an easy mutual attraction. If they get involved (I'm thinking of one married couple—a former model and the owner of a gym, respectively) the Faun will be inspired by the Pixie's healthy sexual appetites and self-confidence, while she will appreciate his gentle, youthful energy. Passions may not run extra hot between these two, but a pleasant, lasting relationship can evolve.

PIXIE *(Female)* + VAMPIRE *(Male)*

This unlikely combo isn't the ideal choice for either partner. Pixies aren't judgmental by nature, but she won't feel as if she ever really knows the Vampire and this can be agitating for her. He's all about disguises and presenting an image and she's much more open about who she is. They might have some fun on a few dates, but it's really more of a novelty for both of them. Fairies, who are somewhat like Pixies, maintain a darker edge, so it's not impossible for one to stay with a Vampire for a longer time, especially if they evolve into a Vamp. But this isn't the case with Pixies, who usually remain true to their upbeat natures throughout their lives. A Vampire may become so enchanted with a Pixie that he will eventually recognize her need to see who he really is. He may then reveal his most guarded feelings to her and possibly transform into a Centaur or even a Werewolf. If this happens it is more likely that they can create a lasting relationship.

PIXIE *(Female)* + WEREWOLF *(Male)*

Although the Werewolf has a dark side like the Vampire, he is very appealing to the Pixie, who admires his creative mind and gentle manner. Because of her own happy, sometimes naïve view of life, she may not see the darker aspects of who he is at first. Whereas the Vampire flaunts his darkness, the Werewolf's dark side is perhaps more powerful by nature of its being so hidden. A reformed Werewolf who is able to stay away from substance abuse can make a wonderful mate for a Pixie, or almost any creature. Robert Downey Jr. and his wife, Pixie/Hobby producer Susan Downey (née Levin), are good examples of this. Susan, whose logical Hobby traits made her aware of what she was dealing with, had to put her foot down, but it was what was needed to set this Werewolf on the road to become a Werewood.

 ## MERMAID *(Female)* + CENTAUR *(Male)*

The Centaur is less susceptible to the Mermaid's allure than other types are, and this is exactly why she is interested in him. He'll keep her on her toes trying to impress him, and although he'll acknowledge her beauty and talents, he is usually too caught up in his creative pursuits to give her the attention she craves. Of course, if he finally gives her what she wants, she may lose interest in him. Their dynamic works best when the Centaur remains true to his nature and unwittingly provides his Mermaid with the challenge she loves. They are a magnetic couple and achieve a great deal of fame and fortune together.

Marilyn Monroe and Arthur Miller might have fared better if Marilyn was pure Mermaid and less Fairy, as she would have been strong enough to endure whatever stressors the relationship was exposed to.

 ## MERMAID *(Female)* + TREE ELF *(Male)*

Mermaids and Tree Elves don't usually frequent the same places; if they do, their outer differences may prevent them from getting to know each other. However, the Tree Elf is much more extroverted than the Urban, and his physical attraction to the Mermaid may override his judgment about the fact that she isn't the most down-to-earth companion. She might not take his healing abilities entirely seriously and may find his style too New Age for her taste, but she'll like how open he is with his affection and emotions. There is a lot of fun to be had between these two, even if their pairing does not last forever.

A well-matched Mermaid/Tree Elf couple I know have a very clear arrangement. She charms, he caretakes. She boosts her self-esteem through her acting career and he is a happy acupuncturist who cooks the meals and shares in the child-rearing. In this case, they'll probably be together always.

MERMAID *(Female)* **+ URBAN ELF** *(Male)*

Most Mermaids and Urban Elves run in very different circles, and even if their paths do cross, the introverted Urban may not get up the nerve to approach the diva of the forest. She tends to notice the flashier types and may not pay much attention to him even if he does make a subtle move. It would be to the Mermaid's advantage to consider an Urban Elf who does manage to seek her out. If he makes it this far, he is probably less introverted than some of his fellows, and Urbans do have a lot to offer. Their elegance, taste, intellect, and sexual prowess make them good companions for the demanding Mermaid if she gives one a chance. He in turn will need to reserve some of his harsh judgments and allow her to be her outgoing, glittering self.

The Urban/Mermaid couple I know argue often and both tend to be a bit stubborn. (Urban Elves, though they appear passive, are very strong-minded.) What keeps these two together is probably a hot sex life and constant intellectual stimulation.

MERMAID *(Female)* **+ GARDEN ELF** *(Male)*

Basically every Mermaid needs at least one Garden Elf friend at her side in some capacity to make sure her hair and makeup are perfect and her clothes are flattering. He may criticize her occasional narcissism and rudeness behind her back but still seeks out her company. She's just too fun and glamorous for most Garden Elves to resist. In turn, she will be enamored with him. They can have a lot of fun together and look really great doing it. If things turn romantic they are likely to bond for years, if not for life.

Lots of young Mermaid divas can't resist the pretty Garden Elf, especially if they're both pop singers (many of them are—think Vanessa Hudgens and Zac Efron).

A fictional older Mermaid/younger Garden Elf combination is sexy diva Samantha and sweet glamour-boy Smith from *Sex and the City*.

MERMAID *(Female)* + WOODSMAN *(Male)*

This is a very compatible match. The confident Woodsman won't feel threatened by the Mermaid's attention-seeking ways. In fact, he may appreciate them. He doesn't need to actively pursue the spotlight—he gets noticed easily even if he is quiet. He can sit back and enjoy watching his Mermaid shine in a crowd of admirers. The Mermaid in turn finds the Woodsman quite irresistible. Her only challenge will be that she sometimes gets impatient with his even-tempered personality and may even accuse him of being boring. She'll have to give up the emotional thrill-seeking of her youth in order to fully appreciate the gifts of this pairing.

The Mer-shee Angelina Jolie and her Woodsman Brad Pitt present the ultimate example of this combination. They have both sublimated some of their narcissism into caring for a brood of children, as well as through altruistic acts in the world outside their large, partially adopted family.

MERMAID *(Female)* **+ MERMAN** *(Male)*

In spite of being classified together, these two are very different types. He is laid back while she is high powered. He is casual while she is glam. He likes nature and she likes bling. He is down to earth while she is always shooting for the stars. Although she is named for the sea, she may or may not be drawn to water and nature, at least not in the way he is. However, some Mermaids who have grown up on beaches and learned to surf at a young age may choose to build their identity around the ocean. Their long, flowing hair and fit bodies can be best featured on a beach landscape, and they will work this to its maximum potential. If the Mermaid is a beach diva she may choose a Merman to complete the picture. But Mermaids can be fickle—they not only want to experience a lot of different relationships but also like to change their image on a regular basis. The Mermaid may move on from her bewildered Merman when she becomes restless with the beach diva persona she has created.

I knew many of these couples when I was in high school in the San Fernando Valley. While they got along well in high school, going surfing on weekends and making out at lunchtime, they often didn't end up together. When Mermaids started wanting more than a cute date and seeking financial stability, the Mermen usually dropped out of the picture. While a Faun will understand the Mermaid's need for attention and bling (even if he can't provide it), the Merman will just be confused by her desires or else ignore them.

MERMAID *(Female)* + GIANT *(Male)*

Mermaids are likely to do well with Giants because the Giant is patient with her somewhat self-absorbed ways, and she is able to ignore his occasional bouts of self-pity, knowing eventually she can charm him out of it. He will be a loving partner for her, giving himself entirely, and even if she finds other creatures attractive she is unlikely to meet a more stable and devoted mate. This match is dependent on her developing the maturity to settle down with one creature.

The Mermaid/Giant couple I know don't have the most balanced of relationships. She seems to dominate, but he is quite content to support her at every turn. She is able to make him glow with happiness and he provides her with a safe, if cluttered, haven where she feels as if she is the center of his tchotchke-filled universe. (For one thing, there are lots of porcelain mermaids in his giant aquarium!)

MERMAID *(Female)* + SATYR *(Male)*

A Mermaid and a Satyr can have very exciting sexual chemistry. Their voracious appetites extend beyond sex and they can also have a lot of fun eating, drinking, socializing, and experiencing cultural events together. This connection can be so powerful that it overrides their inherent mistrust of each other. The Mermaid and Weregirl are the only types that really worry the Satyr. He sees that they are as capable of manipulating other creatures as successfully as he does. But he is also turned on by a challenge. A Mermaid has little patience for Satyrs, especially as she matures and sees the Goats for what they are. Still, she may choose to stay with one for a while to enjoy the sensual pleasures of the relationship. If the Satyr is a lot older than the Mermaid and slowing down in his sexual pursuits of other creatures, they can have a lasting, dynamic, and long-term connection.

Hollywood is full of this type of couple. Young Mermaid starlets may charm older producer Satyrs into long-term relationships that reform the Satyr and establish him as a happily monogamous creature. The constant power struggle between them can actually assure longevity rather than destroying it.

Catherine Zeta-Jones's marriage to Michael Douglas fits into this category. On meeting her, Douglas, twenty-five years her senior, presented Zeta-Jones with one of the best pick-up lines known to Satyrs, "I want to father your child." However, in Woodsman fashion, he actually went on to follow up on this.

 MERMAID *(Female)* **+ HOB** *(Male)*

An aggressive Hob can catch a Mermaid if he sets his mind to it. His power and wealth are the lures that draw her in, but he has to be able to accept her flirtatious ways with others or she'll feel claustrophobic in the relationship and leave him for a more understanding Woodsman or a bad-ass Satyr. If they find a way to work things out they can create a stunning home environment in which to raise a family and entertain guests. The good life is theirs for the taking. They just have to make sure they pay as much attention to the quality of their communication as they do to the quality of their forest real estate.

An attorney Hob I dated briefly is now happily settled with a Mermaid MAW (model/actress/whatever), as he likes to call her. My insecurities and worries agitated him because they reminded him of his own, but he finds her confidence reassuring, since she has chosen to be with him. When we first went out he blatantly checked out every Mermaid in the room and proudly disclosed that he rated female creatures with his teenage son. I was mortified, but any Mermaid worthy of her name would either just ignore both these things or make sure they didn't occur or get mentioned in her presence.

Woody Allen's relationship to actress Scarlett Johannson, though not romantic, epitomizes the dynamic between a smart Mermaid-loving, self-effacing Hob and the creature he worships as his muse.

MERMAID *(Female)* **+ FAUN** *(Male)*

These two can engage in easy banter and light-hearted flirting, but the powerful Mermaid will ultimately intimidate the Faun, and he will rarely approach her for more than a casual encounter. If she finds him attractive she will seduce him and then just as quickly move on. As cute, youthful, and charming as Fauns can be they just don't always live up to the demands of the image-conscious, sexually voracious Mermaid. This combination has a chance of working when the Mermaid is a good deal older than the Faun. He'll look up to her as a mentor, and she'll enjoy his company and youth. In fact, Mermaids are probably most successful at dating much younger creatures, although Pixies can also make this work.

The Mermaid/Faun couple I know do well because he is not threatened by her beauty, her skills, or her attention-seeking ways. She is a few years older than he is and less libidinous than she was in her youth, so they are well matched sexually. The Faun, a grade-school teacher, happily lets his Mermaid bask in the spotlight as a professional classical musician, and she allows him space to relax and do his own Faunish things, like working out and watching sports on television. Because she has the freedom to sparkle in the eyes of others she doesn't need his eyes on her at every moment, allowing him to take care of his own needs. Fauns seem rather passive, but they are actually quite independent and are happy being alone for long stretches of time. These two get along well while maintaining their separate lives.

MERMAID *(Female)* **+ VAMPIRE** *(Male)*

"Who is this creature and why are we dating?" the Mermaid and Vampire may think as they sit across from each other. They are both extravagant attention seekers and they just can't begin to compete. It's far too much trouble. Unfortunately it's hard to see how this one can work out. If you know a Vampire and Mermaid who have made it last (I don't), ask them their secret!

MERMAID *(Female)* **+ WEREWOLF** *(Male)*

Mermaids like to flirt with Werewolves (who don't they like to flirt with?), but they might not want to take things further. The Werewolf can appear too grungy and depressed for the sparkling Mermaid. While some types are drawn to his hidden darkness, she is wary of it. Some Werewolves can be real geniuses, but a Mermaid usually won't stay around long enough to recognize this quality. Conversely, Werewolves can fall hard for the alluring Mermaid. She should be warned not to reject him too harshly or there can be dire consequences.

This pairing is not by any means hopeless. A Mermaid whose maternal nature is stimulated by the somewhat bedraggled, melancholy Werewolf can make a positive difference in his life, and she will be rewarded by his response. He can become the loyal, loving, and quite brilliant partner of her dreams.

One of the best marriages I know involves an evolved Mermaid and reformed Werewolf. She is so in love that she is happy to give up some of the spotlight in exchange for nurturing him. He is inspired by her to keep himself together. They have also made really cute babies!

TESS *(Female)* + CENTAUR *(Male)*

Centaurs are masculine enough for the highly feminine Tess. They appreciate her womanly curves and nurturing personality. The artistic Centaur needs a mate who can encourage him and comfort him while he creates his masterpiece. The Tess is not competitive with the Centaur and can give herself fully to him. She achieves so much satisfaction from their relationship that she does not usually feel the need to go out and prove herself in other ways. That said, Tesses usually have rich lives outside of their connections to their partners. I know a Tess who is a devoted mother and friend and holds a nursing job while still maintaining a loving marriage to her challenging Centaur husband.

TESS *(Female)* + TREE ELF *(Male)*

Tree Elves see the similarity between the Tess and Dryad. They admire the kind, nurturing traits of the Tess and her sensitivity to others. The Tess is somewhat steadier than the Dryad, and the Tree Elf finds this quite soothing to his high-strung temperament. The Tess likes the Tree Elf for his kind, outgoing manner and his altruistic interests. She can be comfortable with his flirtatious ways with others as long as he returns to her at the end of the day. These two are likely to make it for the long haul and often add offspring into the picture, as they parent well together. I've met a number of examples of this type of couple in the world of the healing arts.

TESS *(Female)* + URBAN ELF *(Male)*

There can be a lot of sexual tension between these two types. The Urban Elf is often attracted to the Tess physically, but her vulnerability may remind him too much of the part of himself he doesn't want to expose. In turn, she may not like his rigid façade; she prefers a warmer creature. They might get together based on sexual curiosity but this probably won't last unless she plays it very cool and he heats up. Another way this can work is if he has Faunish tendencies. The gentle Faun qualities can modify the Urban Elf edge and make this combination male a good, supportive companion for the Tess. After struggling through a number of difficult relationships with Mermen and Centaurs, my Tess friend settled down to start a family with just such an Urban Faun.

TESS *(Female)* + GARDEN ELF *(Male)*

Tesses and Garden Elves are usually not the best match. She wants more substance and he wants a somewhat more active partner. His occasionally sharp tongue puts her off right away. He may get together with her for comfort and she with him for security, but it is unlikely that the relationship will develop beyond these mutual needs. Sometimes, though, comfort and security can prove enough for both these types. One Tess and Garden Elf couple I know continue to break up and get back together. She has two adopted children and a career as a teacher to keep her busy and content while the relationship fluctuates.

TESS *(Female)* + **WOODSMAN** *(Male)*

Most Tesses are shy and, as mentioned, most Woodsmen are not particularly aggressive in seeking mates. The Woodsman tends to like a
somewhat more extroverted type, and the Tess prefers a bit more
introverted partner. However, a bold Tess who approaches a Woodsman may find that she gains a happy relationship; I've seen it happen.
If the Tess makes the first move, the Woodsman will most likely follow her lead. Ultimately they may grow apart over time, and if they
have children they may place emphasis on their family over their intimate relationship. It will take a concerted effort on both their parts to
keep the romance alive.

TESS *(Female)* + **MERMAN** *(Male)*

The Merman and the Tess seem quite different, but they are actually
very suited to each other. Both have the ability to focus intently on
what is important to them and then come back together, restored and
refreshed by their separate experiences. The Merman appreciates that
the Tess is loving but not clingy, and the Tess likes the Merman's
strength and calm.

I know one such couple that lives by the beach with their two
children. The Tess is responsible for most of the parenting, a task she
wholeheartedly embraces. She may even be able to lure her Merman
away from his watery lover more often than any other female creature.

TESS *(Female)* **+ GIANT** *(Male)*

This couple will begin to speak and move and even look like each other over time. They tend to be almost inseparable and often arrange their lives so that they can eat, sleep, work, and play together. They can communicate without many words and often finish each other's sentences. Both are rather domestic and emphasize the comforts of their home. Many Giant couples decide to have children together and they make loving parents. They do argue but it is mostly rather harmless disagreements, followed by some Giant retreating and Tess appeasing.

A Giant/Tess couple I know are often squabbling or giving each other the silent treatment, but ultimately they are quite devoted and are raising their children well, although most of the work falls on her shoulders.

TESS *(Female)* **+ SATYR** *(Male)*

The fact that the Satyr and Tess are not usually attracted to each other is a positive thing. She isn't his type and he's not hers. Her gentle nature does not pose enough of a challenge for him, and his aggressive seduction techniques are like a flashing sign reading DANGER for her. She can sum him up at one glance, and he sees that she sees him for what he is. The guilt this induces in him causes him to hurry away, tail between his legs. She may feel somewhat rejected if she has to see him hitting on her friends, but ultimately she should be relieved. Neither needs to take this lack of chemistry personally.

TESS *(Female)* **+ HOB** *(Male)*

A Hob often needs the kind of attention only a Tess can provide. One Hob I know relaxes in the comfort of his Tess's arms after she has fed him a lovely home-cooked meal. This is the perfect remedy for a long, hard day of work. The Tess can be satisfied with this relationship as long as her Hob treats her with respect and pays attention to her needs as well.

TESS *(Female)* **+ FAUN** *(Male)*

The Tess and Faun are quite suited to each other if they can both get over their initial reserve. The Tess is a born caretaker and the Faun is perpetually childlike in certain ways. She can be quite nurturing and calming for him. He can provide her with companionship and kindness. They may not have the most passionate of connections, but it can be strong, stable, and loving like it is for at least one pair I know.

TESS *(Female)* **+ VAMPIRE** *(Male)*

The Vampire can take advantage of the Tess, so she must keep her wits about her when it comes to this creature. He can be essentially exploitative, unless he has done a lot of self-examination, and will take whatever she has to give. She may find him alluring, but she can also be put off by his ostentatious manner. This is probably a good thing; it can keep her from giving too much of herself too soon. I've seen this work once or twice. A reformed Vampire with a strong conscience can make a potentially successful mate for a Tess if she first learns to take care of herself around him.

TESS *(Female)* **+ WEREWOLF** *(Male)*

A Werewolf and a Tess will probably feel an immediate attraction. He senses that she will accept him as he is and this is a big turn-on for him. She'll also sense his nonjudgmental attitude and this will bring out her sexual confidence. They may get together quickly and find themselves deeply involved in a short time. When his darker side emerges she will usually be able to handle it quite gracefully and won't be shocked by it. This response will be healing for him and he may be able to overcome his addictions with her help. One Tess/Werewolf couple I know decided not to start a family because they were both aware that he would need most of her energy focused on him to keep them together. As long as such a dynamic works for the Tess, this pair can make a happy life for themselves.

BANSHEE *(Female)* **+ CENTAUR** *(Male)*

The Centaur may be the Banshee's favorite type. His creativity matches hers, as does his passion. However, the Banshee's passion is usually focused primarily on her love interest; only later does she channel that passion into creative expression. The Centaur's passion is for his art, and although it can be directed toward his partner in a sexual way, he is not seeking intimacy in the same way the Banshee is. This can be very frustrating for her. Also, the Centaur may feel threatened if the Banshee is more successful with her creative expression than he is. She probably *will* have success because Banshees are often prodigies in their chosen field while Centaurs can be late bloomers who don't find their perfect form of expression until later in life. Her success may cause him to turn inward even more in order to find inspiration. She won't understand his insecurity because she probably admires his artistry so much—it's a big part of why she loves him. An older Centaur who has already established himself may be better able to handle a precocious young Banshee.

This is the case with a couple I know. The older Centaur screenwriter was married for years to a Mermaid. When she died he spent a long time alone until he met a feisty, passionate Banshee almost twenty years his junior. At first he was intimidated because she was so smart and talented, and she wasn't sure she wanted to date someone who reminded her so much of her father. However, they ultimately couldn't resist each other and are happy together to this day.

 ## BANSHEE *(Female)* **+ TREE ELF** *(Male)*

Banshees and Tree Elves are a common pairing. He is one of the few types that is not in the least threatened by her wildness. She'll like his touchy-feely style, and contrary to her stubborn nature she'll usually welcome his suggestions. He may advise her on ways she can heal herself. She'll sense that he speaks from a place of real compassion, and may blossom for a time. Trouble brews when the Banshee anger flares. This is a natural part of her personality and is deeply connected to her creative expression, but the Tree Elf may find it off-putting. He's not as emotionally repressed as the Urban Elf, but he is still uncomfortable with the darker side of feelings. He may withdraw, causing her to get even more upset. They'll have to do some difficult psychological and spiritual work to heal their relationship, but both have the depth and emotional intelligence to make it succeed if they really want it to.

A Tree I know had just broken up with his longtime Dryad

girlfriend, an artist and therapist, when he met my Banshee friend at a free-form expressive dance workshop. Over the course of several weeks he danced intimately with a variety of female creatures, including my Banshee. One by one, he asked all his partners out to dinner after class, invited them to his house, and took their photographs, but he did not sleep with any of them, as a Satyr would have done. All of these females knew each other and discussed the experience they'd had with the Tree. My friend was wary of him and made a decision not to fall for him as some of the others seemed to have done. He persistently asked her out to dinner and she finally went, but guardedly. At last he told her how much he liked her.

"You've been running energy with all my friends," she said, using typical Tree Elf language that he would be sure to understand.

He admitted she was right.

"You don't seem in a place to get seriously involved."

He agreed. Immediately after this he invited her, a Fairy, and a Dryad to his home for a small dinner party. He had candles, flowers, wine, and a variety of organic salads for his guests. The Dryad fell for the seduction and later expressed her feelings for him in the sweet and vulnerable way that Dryads are wont to do. He told her that he thought she was beautiful but that he didn't have those feelings for her, and she was quite distraught. The Fairy encouraged my Banshee to get involved with him, saying she sensed feelings between them. Luckily my Banshee did not fall for his seduction—she suspects he is actually a Tree Goat—but he still hasn't given up.

The true Tree Elf I once lived with got together with a Banshee after we broke up. I had actually introduced him to her while we were together. Although they fought as passionately as we had, I think they probably made love even more passionately and seemed to understand each other on a deeper level. While he and I are nothng more than polite MySpace friends these days, he and the Banshee maintain a close bond.

WOOD NYMPH SEEKS CENTAUR

BANSHEE *(Female)* + URBAN ELF *(Male)*

The cool demeanor of the Urban Elf can be attractive to a Banshee, who is interested in breaking through the boundaries of other creatures. He in turn may respond to her passionate nature since it reflects a hidden part of himself. She will think that he is opening up to her, and he may do so during make-out sessions. However, the Banshee may ultimately push an Urban Elf so far outside of his comfort zone that he will become increasingly cold with her. When she reacts in full Banshee style he will recoil, snarl, and flee, leaving her bereft but artistically inspired. There isn't too much hope for these very different creatures.

I know a Banshee who has dated quite a number of these Elves, some for long periods of time. She is always attracted to their intelligence, their small, stylish glasses, and their sharp shoes. She likes how they are into sex almost as much as she is, and their apparent repression allows her the pleasing opportunity to tease it out of them. However, after several of these relationships, she is now bent on finding a Giant or a Centaur for the long haul.

BANSHEE *(Female)* + GARDEN ELF *(Male)*

Garden Elves admire and respect Banshees. This Elf will often be solicitous of a Banshee's needs and will devote himself to her in an almost worshipful way. She in turn can rely on him for deep support and encourage him in his endeavors. They will share a strong mutual affection, but things rarely become sexual between them. Because they are both vulnerable in the realm of romantic relationships this can be to their advantage; they may form a long-lasting bond not threatened by the challenges of romance.

My best Banshee friend divides her time between me and her Garden Elf. When she doesn't want to deal with Wood Nymph neuroses (Banshees understand it and are usually patient, but they also have enough of their own) she can count on him for the same devotion sans the high anxiety. She bolsters both of us with her kick-ass strength.

BANSHEE *(Female)* **+ WOODSMAN** *(Male)*

A Woodsman usually doesn't mind high-maintenance creatures, but Banshees can be a bit much even for him. She may find him cute but somewhat superficial for her tastes. Their relationship will often start as a sexual encounter that neither expects to go very far. However, sometimes the chemistry between these two overrides their initial judgments and they may continue to see each other. Over time a relationship may grow. The Banshee may soften and let down her guard around the calming Woodsman energy, and, inspired by her, he may become more of a risk taker. After their relationship is solidified they may even set out to change the world together.

I'll have to refer back to Brad Pitt and Angelina Jolie on this one, as she is almost as much Banshee as Mermaid, or certainly used to be when she was younger. One look at the pictures of the blond Woodsman and tattooed Mer-shee in bed with their numerous natural and adopted children or hurrying down airport runways with their brood tells the story better than the proverbial thousand words.

BANSHEE *(Female)* **+ MERMAN** *(Male)*

Banshee intensity doesn't scare the Merman, who is used to the unpredictable ways of the ocean. His laid-back manner can be comforting to her. However, she often demands some level of conflict to inspire her, so she can get easily bored with this easygoing creature. If she erupts in anger trying to engage him in her drama, he won't take the bait and will calmly retreat. This can cause her even more frustration. The best prognosis for this couple is for the Banshee to immerse herself in the Merman's natural world, where she can find all the challenges, inspiration, and adrenaline she craves and he can continue to enjoy what he loves most. One Banshee I know became so soothed by her Merman that she changed into a Dryad!

BANSHEE *(Female)* + GIANT *(Male)*

While Giants are usually charmed by the Wood Nymph's emotionality, they can be intimidated by the Banshee. A Giant may not approach a Banshee, but he will definitely see and value wild Banshee beauty and often admire her from afar. She is too caught up in her current passion to pay much attention to him. If they do become close she will respect him and appreciate his taste, but he will hardly know what to do with her if he gets her. The Banshee may need to be involved with a more assertive type. The odds are somewhat against them romantically, although artistically they can potentially make beautiful music together.

Still, certain Giants can be the best, most calming mates for tumultuous Banshees, and a Banshee can certainly light a Giant up. I know a Banshee/Giant couple who are made for each other. Since they've been together, she rarely rants or raves, and he has a sparkle in his eye and a spring in his step. He's the only one who really appreciates the intensely emotional female singers/songwriters she loves, and she *is* the intensely emotional female singer/songwriter he loves most.

BANSHEE *(Female)* + SATYR *(Male)*

The chemistry between a Banshee and any Satyr or Satyr combination type is palpable. Because they are both so sexual, they may find themselves involved very quickly. The Satyr won't be able to resist the challenge of the Banshee, who has all the depth and passion he is constantly seeking outside of himself. The problem is that the Banshee really doesn't want a purely physical connection. She is seeking a much deeper emotional and even spiritual component, although she might not admit it. Ultimately, the Satyr will feel inadequate in her presence and scamper off in search of a less ferocious and demanding creature. If this happens, she'll turn the experience into a powerful song or other work of art, so all will not be lost.

One of my best Banshees had a tumultuous experience with a Tree Goat whom she met at a music festival. He approached her and danced in intimate and seductive ways with her. The next day, they found themselves alone in the woods, rolling on the ground and making out wildly. The chemistry between them was powerful, as they are both quite sensual and sexually uninhibited.

A few days later the Tree Goat showed up with a woman whom he introduced as his girlfriend. The Banshee was terribly upset and confronted him, as Banshees are wont to do. He apologized, saying they had broken up and that the former girlfriend had shown up at the festival unexpectedly.

"Why did you introduce her as your girlfriend then?" the Banshee demanded.

"I didn't want to make her uncomfortable," he said.

This, of course, was no consolation to my Banshee, who cut herself off from him in the abrupt and ruthless way that Banshees do when their deceptively tender hearts are hurt. Of course, she went on to write a performance piece about it.

BANSHEE *(Female)* + HOB *(Male)*

Banshees are put off by Hobs from the start, but the Hob may be less threatened by the Banshee than other types are. She poses a challenge to him, and he is generally up for a challenge. He will easily recognize her gifts and possible genius and want to encourage or exploit these, depending on what kind of Hob he is. He can be a good partner for her in life and/or business. If he is exploitative she will usually sense it with her sharp instincts and reject him, but young Banshees who have been hurt in some way as children may fall prey to exploitation quite easily. On the other hand, if he is a loving Hob, the young Banshee may not always recognize the gifts he has to offer, especially if she is preoccupied with chasing inaccessible Satyrs or Centaurs. A conscientious Hob and a mature Banshee, like a manager and choreographer I know, can make a good, if odd, match.

BANSHEE *(Female)* + FAUN *(Male)*

Banshees tend to scare Fauns, but some will admire this fascinating type. For her part, a Banshee will be able to detect a Faun's ambiguous sexuality right away and may be put off by it. After all, she is attracted to creatures who are clear about what they want, even if it's not what she wants. Still, if these two ever get around to spending time together, they might be able to learn something from each other. The Faun may get in touch with his inner passion through his association with a Banshee, and the Banshee may be calmed and comforted by the Faun's soft-spoken, easygoing manner. He's a good, compassionate listener, even if he doesn't contribute a lot to the conversation, and she is always brimming with intense thoughts and feelings.

The Faun/Banshee couple I knew broke off their engagement when he got cold feet and felt she was demanding too much of him. She went on to get involved with a female Brownie and he met a much younger Fairy, but he continued to mentor the Banshee's son from a previous relationship. In his new relationship, the Faun continued to flirt casually with both male and female creatures, but the Fairy—unlike a Banshee—was able to keep any upset this might have caused her to herself.

 ## BANSHEE *(Female)* + VAMPIRE *(Male)*

Not every type can understand a Vampire as well as a Banshee. She will recognize his elaborate persona as a disguise but she will also appreciate its glamour. Her tattoos, extreme hairstyle, and piercings are her own form of disguise. For both of them, these trappings have important symbolic meaning and are not just superficial. The Banshee and Vampire can go a long way on their compatible aesthetics. They'll often enjoy the same music, or at least find that their interests overlap. They like the same nighttime world, and they appreciate edgy fashion, art, films, and literature. A challenge they may face is that the Vampire tends to be quite cool or even cold, while the Banshee runs extremely hot. Although they can enjoy an uninhibited sexual connection, the emotional intimacy between them is harder to achieve. The Banshee can become too unpredictable and demanding for the Vampire, unconsciously pushing him away. He will become increasingly cold and they may part. If a Banshee wants a relationship with a Vampire she'll have to tame her emotions and he'll have to open his heart. Tori Amos's relationship with Nine Inch Nails' Trent Reznor fell into this category. The relationship inspired much powerful songwriting from Tori after it came to an end.

Another example also comes from the world of rock music. PJ Harvey is a rare Banshee/Vamp combination whose romance with Vampire Nick Cave proved creatively productive, although it did not last either.

BANSHEE *(Female)* + WEREWOLF *(Male)*

Banshees get along famously with Werewolves. She loves his bedraggled but somehow always stylish appearance, his interest in the arts, and the dark side she knows lurks beneath the surface. She is not at all threatened by his addictive behaviors, and is often, in fact, attracted to them. He, of course, can fully appreciate her darkness as well. He's less fickle than a Satyr and less easily threatened than a Centaur. When his dark side reveals itself he knows she will not reject him for it. He may even find that he needs to indulge in destructive behaviors on a less regular basis. Rather than losing interest in him when he does this, the Banshee will fall even more deeply in love with her Werewolf.

I know a Banshee/Werewolf couple who met in A.A. meetings and were immediately attracted to each other's edgy, wounded personas. Because they were both in recovery, they were able to take this dark attraction and turn it into a healthy, loving relationship.

HOBBY *(Female)* + CENTAUR *(Male)*

A Hobby can help a Centaur along the road to success by providing the organizational and promotional skills he may not be able to find in himself. Through this kind of work relationship, love may develop between them. A good, solid Hobby can be the key to a Centaur's happiness if he isn't distracted by a Mermaid or Wood Nymph. Other less serious problems can arise if he gets so absorbed in his work that he fails to give her the attention she needs. She's not as high maintenance with males as other types (although she can act out a bit with females), and she has her own work to keep her busy, but like any creature she wants to feel appreciated. The Centaur must show how much he values this creature if he's going to keep the relationship alive.

One couple I know were able to make this work when the Hobby gave up some of her business duties for more creative pursuits the way her artist boyfriend had. Then there was less frustration between them.

HOBBY *(Female)* + TREE ELF *(Male)*

On the surface this seems like an unlikely pairing, and it's not very common. But I do know a Hobby who is very happy with her Tree Elf waiter boyfriend. He is laid back enough not to mind her forceful personality and she relies on his easygoing nature to help her unwind after a hard day at the office. She's not threatened by his occasional flirtations with other female creatures because she's too busy climbing the business ladder and enjoying the validation she receives in that arena. Sometimes opposites do attract!

HOBBY *(Female)* + URBAN ELF *(Male)*

Urban Elves are not intimidated by strong female creatures, so the Hobby's success in her career will only enhance his interest in her. In turn, she'll like how organized and efficient he is. They are both quite sensitive and probably won't step on each other's toes too often. Sexually, the Hobby may not be quite as adventuresome as the Urban Elf (not many female types are) but he will usually be able to accept this difference between them. He tends to think of his interest in sex as slightly excessive and is a bit apologetic about it anyway. He will be attentive to her in bed and out. They can enjoy a long, close relationship, although they usually won't choose to bring little creatures into the picture. They are both too focused on their careers for this. The upside is that they'll have the time and resources to put the emphasis on their relationship, like my Hobby/Urban friends who are keeping it fresh and interesting even as they grow old together.

HOBBY *(Female)* + GARDEN ELF *(Male)*

There usually isn't much potential for romance here. The Garden Elf can relate best to the Hobby platonically as he tries to help her with her relationships or career. He'll be more gracious and gentle with her than with other types because she isn't threatening to him and he recognizes her underlying sensitivity. She'll welcome his suggestions and he'll happily celebrate her success with her.

In spite of the rarity of this combination, I do know one such couple that has been married for years. They run a hair salon together—he cuts, she does the books. They also have a child they love and nurture.

HOBBY *(Female)* + WOODSMAN *(Male)*

Hobbies and Woodsmen may not encounter each other very much in the dating world when they are young, but as they mature they are more likely to hook up. If they decide to settle down, they can have a very happy family life. She'll usually be the one going to work and he'll stay home with the little creatures. She'll bring home the paycheck and he'll cook the meals. He'll charm her into making love with him, even when she's tired after a long day, and she'll usually feel better for it. They might argue about the messy house but that's usually the worst of their conflicts. Their little ones will usually grow up quite well adjusted since both parents are doing what they enjoy best.

I know quite a few happy Hobby/Woodsman couples that have started families together.

HOBBY *(Female)* + MERMAN *(Male)*

The Hobby and the Merman aren't usually in the same place at the same time. They face the same challenges that the Urban Elf and Merman face. However, the Urban Elf's temperament is somewhat more artistic, so she will be more likely to appreciate the Merman through an artist's eyes. The Hobby will examine the Merman's life from a practical prospective and wonder how he is going to pay the bills and when is he going to stop renting and buy a home. For these superficial reasons the Hobby and Merman might never get together, even for a one-night stand. (That's not her thing anyway.) She might be able to help him find a job or represent him as a Realtor if he finally does purchase that beach shack. He might help build her self-confidence if he's in a flirtatious mood. Merman have quite a soothing effect on female creatures when they want to exert their charm.

One Hobby I know was obsessed with Mermen as a teencreature. She didn't want to date anyone else. She was so attractive and somehow exotic to them with her good grades and precise way of dressing that they all had crushes on her, too, but she didn't feel that they really understood who she was, and she ended up settling down with a devoted Hob who shared all her interests.

HOBBY *(Female)* **+ GIANT** *(Male)*

This is a very good match for the Hobby. The gentle Giant is very considerate of her feelings and respects her success without feeling threatened by it. She will value his slow-moving, soft-spoken manner; it is soothing to her. They will probably have a very pleasant, conflict-free courtship. The Giant may withdraw a little when his Hobby stays too long at the office, but she can easily snap him out of it with a bit of snuggling. In the case of one such couple, he wanted children before she did, but she eventually took some time off of work to raise a family with her Giant. I know another Hobby/Giant couple that married in their forties and stayed together until they passed away in their nineties! The romance never died between them.

HOBBY *(Female)* **+ SATYR** *(Male)*

The Satyr can catch the unsuspecting Hobby off guard. She may be going along happily enough, focusing on her career, when he pops up and tries to seduce her. He'll move slowly with her and not flash his tattoos or piercings right away. Over time she may give in to his advances. She'll be more wounded than she appears to be when he moves on. It is probably better for her to avoid this type completely.

Sorry, Satyrs. I know I'm giving you limited options here. Perhaps I'm a bit prejudiced.

HOBBY *(Female)* **+ HOB** *(Male)*

The Hob is organized, efficient, and sensitive like the Urban Elf but he's not quite as nurturing to his partner. He, in turn, needs a creature who nurtures him, and the Hobby's main focus is on her career. They'll both have to compromise a bit to make this work but they have a lot in common, so it is worth the effort. In the bedroom they will have to take turns initiating intimacy or it may wane between them. In spite of their focus on their careers, this pair will probably want little creatures, as Hobs and Hobbies tend to be quite traditional. Whereas the Urban Elf is emotionally, if not professionally, an eternal youth who may feel overwhelmed by the emotional responsibilities of parenthood, and the Faun is the exact opposite—childlike professionally but a potentially devoted parent—the Hob is quite responsible both in his career and as a parent, and he may actually be the one to encourage the Hobby to start a family. If the connection between these two is not romantic, or even if it is, they can also be extremely successful as business partners. They are both easy to find in almost any office environment.

HOBBY *(Female)* **+ FAUN** *(Male)*

Fauns like the Hobby's take-charge approach, and for her he can be a refreshing change from the high-powered Hob or cool metrosexual Urban Elf—two types she is likely to meet most often. The Faun is comfortable with strong females and so he is not threatened if the Hobby makes more money than he does or is in a more powerful position. She's not as athletic as he is but she's not uninterested in sports and probably frequents a gym, too, even if it isn't her favorite pastime.

It's not unheard of for these types to settle into a comfortable life together in which she is the primary breadwinner and he takes care of the kids. This probably isn't the most passionate of relationships, and whatever fire there was in the beginning may cool over time, but it won't be the cause of a split since it probably isn't the priority for either type.

I know one such couple that is happily raising two children together. She works as an artist's agent, while he dabbles in creative projects and cares for the little ones. Although I have caught her rolling her eyes at his childlike behavior, they are quite devoted to each other. A fictional couple that fit this category are lawyer Miranda and bartender Steve from *Sex and the City*.

 ## HOBBY *(Female)* + VAMPIRE *(Male)*

Once again, it may be superficial factors that keep these two creatures apart. The Vampire's extreme style and mannerisms can come across as threatening to most Hobbies, and Hobbies appear too conventional for the image-conscious Vampire. However, there can be a great deal of sexual attraction between these two unlikely creatures. They may not choose to play it out but if they do they will both be in for quite a surprise. The Vampire brings out the Hobby's secret wild side and she might inspire a softer side of him. He may unconsciously recognize that both of them are hiding behind a persona, although his is so much flashier and more obvious. They are both probably afraid of something. If the Vampire and the Hobby overcome their prejudices and learn to trust each other, like one couple I met, they might be able to explore their fears together, both in bed and out, and come to some fascinating truths about themselves.

HOBBY *(Female)* **+ WEREWOLF** *(Male)*

At first the Werewolf seems less strange to the Hobby than the Vampire might, but he exerts a similar kind of pull on her. She probably hasn't been exposed to creatures like him before, so she won't know exactly how to react when he unleashes his darker side. The attraction to him will remain strong but she might be afraid and retreat anyway. The Werewolf may not pursue her at all; he's quite sensitive to rejection and could feel inferior to her from the beginning.

"She seems to have her life so together," one Werewolf said to me about a Hobby he was interested in. "Why would she want to be with a loser like me?" I reassured him, but I wasn't sure how the Hobby in question really felt. Even if she didn't consider him a loser, it's possible that she might not have wanted to take the risk of being with such a changeable sort in the long term.

But there is some hope for these two types. A Hobby attorney acquaintance of mine has been married to her hairdresser Werewolf for years. They have a child and a happy, functional marriage.

 BROWNIE *(Female)* **+ CENTAUR** *(Male)*

A Brownie will flirt with a Centaur when they meet and he'll love her smile, but after they start talking in depth they may find that they don't have a lot in common. Brownies tend to find Centaurs a bit bewildering and exasperating. She is in general a pretty accepting sort, but she doesn't understand his fascination with his work, and this is so important to him that he can lose interest in her rather quickly. Sometimes they can get past this if she takes the time to understand what makes him tick and he learns to see that her smile and strength can be as alluring as his latest creative project.

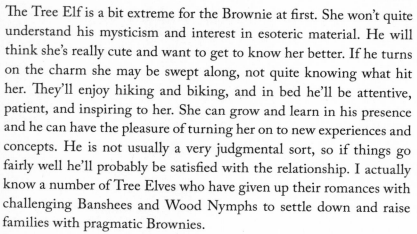

BROWNIE *(Female)* **+ TREE ELF** *(Male)*

The Tree Elf is a bit extreme for the Brownie at first. She won't quite understand his mysticism and interest in esoteric material. He will think she's really cute and want to get to know her better. If he turns on the charm she may be swept along, not quite knowing what hit her. They'll enjoy hiking and biking, and in bed he'll be attentive, patient, and inspiring to her. She can grow and learn in his presence and he can have the pleasure of turning her on to new experiences and concepts. He is not usually a very judgmental sort, so if things go fairly well he'll probably be satisfied with the relationship. I actually know a number of Tree Elves who have given up their romances with challenging Banshees and Wood Nymphs to settle down and raise families with pragmatic Brownies.

BROWNIE *(Female)* **+ URBAN ELF** *(Male)*

The Urban Elf may become defensive around the Brownie. Her shiny smile can seem aggressive to him. She won't share much sexual energy with him, as she rarely does in the beginning with anyone, and the sensitive Elf may take this as a sign that she is rejecting him. She's sharp as a tack mentally but not particularly interested in some of his intellectual pursuits. And she's so athletic! (Urbans tend not to be.) The Brownie might read his defensiveness as coldness and avoid him. If they can get past this initial tension, they might enjoy each other's company for a time, but they don't have much in common. She thinks he's too serious; he may think that her smile is the cover for a certain superficiality (it isn't). She'll want to work out at the gym; he'll want to walk around the city or stretch in his living room. She'll want to go to a fun movie; he'll want to see a foreign film or read a book. He'd like to spend the whole date in bed having sex and she wants to eat a good meal and snuggle. Brownies are a rather specific type that doesn't often combine with other types, but if she's part Urban Elf and he's part Faun, as is the case with one couple I know, her intellectual interests and his less omnipresent sexuality can help to make this combination work.

 BROWNIE *(Female)* **+ GARDEN ELF** *(Male)*

A pleasant rapport can develop between the Brownie and Garden Elf, but there are times when they get on each other's nerves a bit. He doesn't understand her taste (or lack thereof, as he might define it) and she doesn't understand his criticism. They can get frustrated with each other and give up or try to see it through and enjoy the benefits of their relationship—upbeat conversations, thrilling gossip, and a loyal ally when someone turns on either of them.

My Garden Elf yoga teacher (OK, he's a bit of a Tree, too) is always surrounded by Brownies. They absolutely worship him and he basks in the attention. They can all do arm balances in the center of the room and make jokes during class. Afterward they all hang out together. I'm frankly a bit jealous, but I'm too much of a Wood Nymph to even attempt to join the fun.

 BROWNIE *(Female)* **+ WOODSMAN** *(Male)*

The Brownie is a fan of Woodsmen, and her friendly manner can easily endear her to this creature. He'll love her smile and she'll love his masculinity and sweetness. Neither of them will judge the other for being shallow or superficial, while other types may make this judgment about them. They'll enjoy outdoor activities, popular movies, music, and new restaurants together. Their sex life might be slightly predictable, as the Woodsman usually relies on his partner to keep things varied and romantic. The Brownie may not be as interested in this aspect of the relationship as some other types might be. If this is the case, the Woodsman might possibly be sexually tempted by an aggressive Mermaid or Wood Nymph, but his affection for his Brownie can win if she stays focused on his needs. As sexist as this sounds, that is part of the deal when you're with a Woodsman, she-creatures! If you want a more conscientious creature, talk to a Tree Elf or Giant!

The Brownie who I had a falling out with years ago is happily married to a former Satyr who became a Woodsman when they had their children.

 ## BROWNIE *(Female)* + MERMAN *(Male)*

Brownies tolerate the Merman's obsession with nature because it involves physical activity—something she too can become obsessive about. She'll love how physically strong he is; he'll love how athletic she is. They will enjoy outdoor activities and meals together. They'll experience pleasant sexual encounters, but this may be less of a priority for them than other things.

I know a Brownie/Merman couple that brings out the best in each other. She's a physical education coach and he's a swim instructor, so they both spend a lot of time around children. They have completed triathlons together. Their friends find them charming and frequently stop by their condo for a beer, some barbecue, and a soak in the hot tub.

BROWNIE *(Female)* + GIANT *(Male)*

This is a very successful combination that can last for years, if not a lifetime. I know of one such couple. The Brownie appreciates the Giant's stability, loyalty, and respectful adoration. It doesn't make her feel claustrophobic or smothered in the least. The Giant likes that she's more predictable than Fairies or Wood Nymphs. The fact that she's not as overtly sexual as these types makes her less intimidating to him. He admires her beauty, strength, and savvy. He rarely if ever insults her, so she doesn't need to show him her vengeful side. She thinks he's loveable and tender, if mildly and even pleasantly eccentric. She may wish he was a bit more physically active, but she probably does enough exercise for two creatures. Their libidos are similarly mild, so she is rarely forced to reject his advances and in turn he rarely mopes around her.

BROWNIE *(Female)* + SATYR *(Male)*

Satyrs like the no-pressure attitude of the Brownie. So many other female types seem ready to pounce emotionally, but the Brownie presents herself as a warm friend who won't burden him with emotional expectations. Soon he'll find himself confiding in her and basking in her good-natured energy and the light from her smile. Eventually this will probably lead to sex, as most Satyr relationships do. He'll know just how to convince her to take their friendship beyond the platonic realm. They can have a lot of fun sexually; Brownies are inspired by the Satyr's lust and she may overcome some of her ennui or general reluctance in bed. Her warmth and charisma will become evident as she grows more secure with him. Unfortunately, her naïveté may allow her to get too attached to the fickle Goat, who has the potential to do her harm. On the other hand, he may realize that he might never again find such a good, solid, understanding friend, and stick around. She'll just have to know that she takes a risk; he may get distracted by other creatures, but if she's patient and not too wounded to accept him, he'll usually come back.

As mentioned, the Satyr who I dated for a year is now happily involved with a kickboxing, kick-ass Brownie. She is less demanding of him than I was, less clingy and emotional. She continues to date two other creatures while she is seeing him, so that he doesn't ever feel too hemmed in. She bounces around, grinning wildly and calling everyone "dude." Never a sad or guilt-inducing look from her! He tells her he loves her and has regular sex with her but doesn't seem to have plans to take it further than that. Although you just never know—there's a day in even a Satyr's life when he may just decide to settle down.

BROWNIE *(Female)* **✝ HOB** *(Male)*

These two types are likely to meet, date, and even settle down together. The Brownie is immediately attracted to the Hob's business skills, confidence, and financial success. He'll like her warmth and easygoing personality. The fact that she doesn't always have an intense passion for something can be seen as a plus for him. He'll find that he has less to compete with for her attention—and Hobs need lots of attention. Both of these types are comfortable with the idea of settling down and starting a family. They'll be able to make a nice, welcoming home together and maintain a loving relationship for years. The only challenge they may face is if the Hob retreats too far into his work, like one businesscreature I know, and his Brownie feels rejected. He'll need to reevaluate his priorities if he wants to hold the relationship together.

BROWNIE *(Female)* **+ FAUN** *(Male)*

Brownies and Fauns are a good match and will usually become instant friends. The outgoing Brownie will flash her smile at the more reserved Faun, laugh at his gentle jokes, and ask him questions about himself. She'll chatter on, and he'll listen attentively; then he will venture to open up, and she'll encourage him all the way. They'll share similar interests like working out at a gym, enjoying outdoor sports, and attending social gatherings. They are both usually physically strong and capable. They have a similar casual style, although the Faun probably spends a little more time grooming himself than the Brownie does. Neither of them are particularly driven by their sexuality, so this aspect of their relationship may take time to develop or it may fall away over time. Some Brownies might feel insulted or neglected by the Faun's lack of interest in sex, but many are actually relieved by it, especially as they get older. When the Brownie and her Faun get into an argument, which is rather rare, they can become so dogmatically positioned that it takes them a while to find a resolution. However, they will usually work it out, and no matter what happens they will probably remain friends forever. This is an unusual stance for the Brownie, who is known for holding grudges with some of the other types.

The couple I know that best typifies this match met at the gym (where else?). They were just friends at first, gently teasing each other while they shared the same weight-lifting machines and enjoying movies and lunches together. Soon things turned romantic, although they kept their relationship a secret for a long time. Brownies are notoriously stealthy even though they appear quite outgoing. The Faun is still a bit evasive about the relationship as is to be expected from his type.

Oh yeah, and if you want a celebrity example, can you say Tom Cruise and Katie Holmes?

BROWNIE *(Female)* ✦ VAMPIRE *(Male)*

The Brownie gets along with a lot of creatures, but she doesn't understand the Vampire at all. She thinks he's just plain weird. He'll sense this from her right away. Just as her radiant smile reveals her warmth to everyone who sees it, her scowl makes it clear when she's not impressed. They inhabit different social circles and work environments, so it's not too likely they'll even meet. If they do, it will take a lot of tolerance on both their parts for them to overcome their initial impressions and prejudices and get acquainted. Even then, the chances are that the rather down-to-earth Brownie and flashy, eccentric Vampire won't make a lasting match.

BROWNIE *(Female)* ✦ WEREWOLF *(Male)*

Although Werewolves are almost as extreme as Vampires, they don't show it at first. They come across as a little shy, rumpled, intelligent, and pleasant. The Brownie will be intrigued by this creature, who may remind her of her father, and the Werewolf will enjoy her company. He's usually a bit passive about the creatures that involve themselves with him, so if she makes the effort he'll go along with it, thinking she's cute and smart. When and if he starts to show the addictive side of his nature she won't be particularly fazed and can generally take it in stride. Sometimes, as is the case with one couple I met, she can even help him to overcome his addictions—that is, if he doesn't push her buttons. If he turns on her aggressively she may not stick around.

VAMP *(Female)* + CENTAUR *(Male)*

A Vamp in love with a Centaur? It's actually very common. While she often applies her creativity to her image rather than to her work, they do share an artistic temperament. He's strong enough to handle her capricious nature. Her mysterious sexuality makes her a perfect muse for him. Centaurs are often too distracted and preoccupied with their work to get very jealous, but the Vamp can bring this out. She doesn't mind a certain amount of jealousy from him; it actually makes her feel appreciated, as long as it doesn't go too far. He'll have to keep it in check or she'll be on her way.

VAMP *(Female)* + TREE ELF *(Male)*

Tree Elves don't judge books by their covers, and if they think a Vamp is attractive they won't dismiss her because of her extreme style. A Vamp, in turn, is likely to be attracted to the Tree Elf because of his open-mindedness and risk-taking ways. He won't try to change her or cramp her style and neither of them is particularly threatened by what is usually harmless attention-seeking from members of the opposite sex. They are both free thinkers and will find a great deal of fascinating material to explore together. Their sex life will be rich and varied. There will usually be some spiritual component to their relationship, as the Tree Elf is naturally a spiritual seeker and the Vamp is open to life's mysteries and is seeking a partner to share them with. They probably won't settle into a conventional lifestyle but, like the Vamp I met online and her gentle Tree Elf beau, they can create a vibrant life together.

VAMP *(Female)* + URBAN ELF *(Male)*

According to a few Urban Elves I've interviewed, the Vamp represents their secret fantasies. She has a dangerous eroticism that this Elf finds intoxicating. She'll be turned on by the sexual power she can wield over him. This is enough to get them together, at least. However, the Urban Elf might not be able to value the Vamp beyond her sexual role. She'll eventually want to be seen as more than the object of his arousal, but he will rarely share his daily life with her. This can cause so much strain on the relationship that it may finally fall apart.

VAMP *(Female)* + GARDEN ELF *(Male)*

A Garden Elf can often find himself enchanted by a Vamp, but she might not be as easily captured. He does have some of that edge she likes, but not quite enough, and she may see her relationship with him as a bit of a lark. ("Wouldn't it be kind of fun to make out with that cute little creature in the ascot?" she'll think.) If she gives this a chance, though, there's a lot of potential. Both these creatures like to attract attention and they will certainly do just that when they go out together. On the other hand, they are both quite shy and can therefore understand this quality in the other. They both spend a lot of time thinking about the image they present, and they have artistic leanings. Although many other creatures find these types sexually appealing, both are actually less overtly sexual than they may appear. They might value cuddling and reading aloud to their partner over wild sex on some nights. This relationship is something to explore. It can be found most often in rock 'n' roll since both these types gravitate to the glamour and power of that world.

VAMP *(Female)* + WOODSMAN *(Male)*

This match is really a bit of a novelty for both parties. The Vamp sometimes likes to experience intimacy with a variety of creatures if she finds them attractive, and the Woodsman is definitely on her list. He'll willingly respond to her advances and they can enjoy each other a great deal. They may not decide to take it to the next level unless one or both of them is interested in changing their type a bit. A Woodsman who feels he's too conventional may want to expand his horizons by becoming a Vampire, but this is usually just a phase influenced by a Vamp. A Vamp who is particularly attracted to a Woodsman may settle into the role of a Night Fairy. The latter transformation is more likely to last than the former and sometimes this combination can evolve—as it did with a fashion designer Vamp I know and her Woodsman actor boyfriend—into a successful long-term relationship.

VAMP *(Female)* + MERMAN *(Male)*

The Merman is not intimidated or shocked by the Vamp, but he's not sure what to make of her, either. She seems to have disassociated herself so much from the natural world that he can't really relate to her. In turn, she finds him a bit boring. They both share a certain spiritual longing, but it takes such different forms that they may not recognize it in each other. However, the Vamp's pagan leanings are not that different from the Merman's water worship. She is more connected to nature than he may perceive at first, and he's deeper and more spiritual than she might think. If they come together around this shared interest they may be able to benefit from a relationship of some kind.

VAMP *(Female)* **+ GIANT** *(Male)*

The Vamp doesn't trust most types very easily, but the Giant is some-one she'll feel comfortable with right away. He'll continue to earn her trust, and their relationship can grow. He'll see all her best qualities and not be threatened by the darker aspects of her nature. She may be able to work out certain unresolved father issues with him. However, when it comes to romance she tends to be attracted to edgier types. If their relationship does evolve in that direction, as it did with one couple I met, he may become upset over the attention she naturally provokes from other male creatures. This will be a difficult challenge for them to overcome.

VAMP *(Female)* **+ SATYR** *(Male)*

The Vamp and Satyr are likely to meet as they both frequent edgy, artsy environments. They also both project a strong sexual vibe that attracts them to each other. The Satyr will feel that he's met his match, but the Vamp is actually much more delicate than she appears. He doesn't think that he can hurt a creature who seems to be so in touch with her dark side and probably has at least a few piercings in sensitive places. Of course, this has nothing to do with how easily she can be hurt. She'll fall hard for all his plays and may think she's met her soul mate. She tends to be mystical like the Dryad and believes in this type of connection. And, in fact, it is not impossible for a Satyr to fall in love for life with a Vamp. I've seen it happen—and last! Their sex-ual chemistry and ability to fearlessly explore the dark side can bond them deeply. It's a chance she may have to take.

VAMP *(Female)* + HOB *(Male)*

"Um. Not," a Hob may say to himself when he first sees the Vamp. Even if he secretly finds her attractive, the Hob might not be able to understand her need for all that body art and makeup. She in turn won't necessarily like his conventional style and loud voice. She won't get his jokes. These two are just basically not suited for each other, and their lack of immediate interest is probably something to be respected and not forced.

But there are always exceptions: Sonny and Cher were a happy Vamp/Hob combo for many years, at least before they fully solidified into their types. (A mature Hob would never have worn those pants and ruffles!)

VAMP *(Female)* + FAUN *(Male)*

She'll seem like someone he can't approach and she'll feel just as intimidated by him. They are both much more shy than they seem and also more accepting. They'll need a good matchmaker if they are even going to have a conversation, and most forest yentas probably won't see much potential here. If these two types do get together—I've found one example—the Vamp is able to stir up the Faun's latent passions and the Faun keeps her calm. This is an unusual but possibly workable match.

VAMP *(Female)* + VAMPIRE *(Male)*

This is a natural match. They'll probably feel a strong kinship right away and get involved sexually almost immediately. They can enjoy many of the same activities, and both love the joint impression they make when they walk into a room. They are both experts at mythologizing themselves. Many female types may actually change into a Vamp when under the spell of a Vampire, although for the most part male types are less likely to make a similar transformation for their Vamp. This is partly because she tends to be more accepting of diversity than the Vampire is. Still, she definitely appreciates the qualities of her own kind and these two together can make a very intriguing couple. Their fights can get vicious, though, and their bond can be broken by these outbursts.

Marilyn Manson and Dita Von Teese's marriage was an example of this coupling. Tim Burton and Helena Bonham Carter are a more successful example. The artist Salvador Dalí, who is known for his shocking imagery and exhibitionistic persona, and his equally provocative wife/muse Gala are a classic couple in this category.

 VAMP *(Female)* **+ WEREWOLF** *(Male)*

The Werewolf is an even better match for the Vamp than the Vampire is, at least at first. Although they share a similar aesthetic and sensibility, the Werewolf can be more gentle than the Vampire, even in his inebriated state, and will probably not act out on others as much as take out his stress on himself. The Vamp can be very loving in these situations and is sometimes able to pull him through. This isn't always the case, however. Sometimes this combination can be dangerous for the Werewolf. The alluring nature of the Vamp can drive him to a self-destructive edge.

WEREGIRL *(Female)* + CENTAUR *(Male)*

Weregirls tend to be quite creative, like their male counterpart, the Werewolf, and they'll be really attracted to this aspect of the Centaur. In turn, he'll like how seductive she is and he won't be afraid of the sometimes wild look in her eye. This pairing can work because they are both able to occupy themselves with activities outside of the relationship. While he devotes himself to the work she admires, she'll be off socializing. Problems arise if she takes this too far. They'll both have to make the relationship their first priority for it to last, and that isn't the easiest task for either of these forest folk, especially if they are young and famous like the Centaur Johnny Depp and Weregirl Winona Ryder.

WEREGIRL *(Female)* + TREE ELF *(Male)*

The empathetic Tree Elf will have a lot of patience with even a wayward Weregirl. The Weregirl, with her natural curiosity for many things, will enjoy learning about the healing arts, nutrition, and spirituality from him. They can have fun together, enjoying the outdoors and talking about their feelings. If the Weregirl succumbs to temptation, the Tree Elf is one of the types best qualified to help her through to the other side. This is the case with a chiropractor Tree Elf and photographer Weregirl I know. They have formed a powerful, loving relationship that is likely to last for a long time.

WEREGIRL *(Female)* + URBAN ELF *(Male)*

One sensitive Urban Elf I know is at his Weregirl's mercy. He plays it cool, but she sees right through him. She can keep up with him intellectually like a female Urban and attract him sexually like a Wood Nymph, and he likes the mysterious puzzle she presents him with. Who is she and how did she become this way? he wonders. In contrast, she is able to sum him up right away, as Weregirls are quite intuitive.

Weregirls may toy with Urban Elves for a while, and some might even honestly fall for an Urban's smarts and his stamina in bed. However, he's usually not quite emotionally passionate enough for her. She likes to feel as if she has engaged the whole creature—not just his body and intellect, but also his soul. He won't be particularly tolerant of any addictions she might have. Urban Elf males aren't usually the most compassionate sorts when they're on the defensive. These two will have a lot of challenges if they decide to give it a go.

WEREGIRL *(Female)* + GARDEN ELF *(Male)*

The Garden Elf can accept and ultimately handle the Weregirl's antics, and she respects him for this. These two creatures can be a force to contend with when they are together. No one is safe from their intuitive and often critical perceptions. They'll have a lot of fun going out together, gossiping, drinking, dancing, and meeting many different kinds of creatures. If things get romantic between these two they have the potential for a long-lasting, always interesting liaison. I know a Weregirl who constantly tested her Garden Elf with flirtations, emotional outbursts, and wild partying. He was so devoted to her that he tolerated it all. The pleasure he gained from her charm outweighed the problems for him. Although she took things too far a number of times, causing a temporary split, they always found their way back to each other.

WEREGIRL *(Female)* + WOODSMAN *(Male)*

Weregirls don't usually gravitate toward Woodsmen. She'll probably make a snap judgment based on his conventional good looks and cheerful demeanor and decide he's not complex enough for her. He might possibly find her attractive, but as usual he'll wait for her to make the first move. If she doesn't initiate it, these two probably won't connect. Woodsmen are instinctively looking for a female creature to raise a family with, and the Weregirl is a bit unstable as a mother unless she deals with some of her hidden issues. If these two find themselves together for a noncommittal quickie they'll probably enjoy it and not suffer any real consequences.

WEREGIRL *(Female)* + MERMAN *(Male)*

Mermen are somewhat suspicious of Weregirls from the start. These gentle, laid-back male creatures don't mind passion and wildness because it reminds them of nature, but they mistrust emotional instability. The Weregirl may dismiss the Merman as not being deep or intelligent enough for her. There may be a physical attraction, but it will probably be short lived. This is not the case with one couple I know; the Merman's influence has turned the Weregirl into a Dryad and they are very happy together.

WEREGIRL *(Female)* + GIANT *(Male)*

The relationship between a Weregirl and a Giant is not unlike her relationship with an Urban Elf. The Giant will be captivated by her charm and mystery and want to understand what makes her tick. The Weregirl enjoys the attention from him and milks it for all that it is worth. She'll be less likely to fall for him than for the Urban, however. The Giant's vulnerability can put her off and even bring out a vicious side. He should be very careful when dealing with this type. The best examples I've found of this pairing are platonic and involve the Giant serving as a mentor and benefactor for the Weregirl.

WEREGIRL *(Female)* + SATYR *(Male)*

These two can practically smell each other across a crowded room. Their attraction will be immediate. They'll be certain to enjoy great sex and a lot of other sensual pleasures together. They also share a certain voracious longing that not every type can understand. Their passion is emotional as well as physical. It isn't easy to sustain this level of intensity, however, and the Weregirl ultimately wants a somewhat more stable partner to give her the security she desires. The Weregirl is one of the only types who has the power to really break a Satyr, and he may feel this in his bones when they meet. It won't discourage him; he'll be too attracted to her to resist and he always likes a challenge anyway.

The tabloids are full of snapshots of wild Weregirls and Satyrs out on the town. How many of these relationships last past the next issue is another story.

184

WEREGIRL *(Female)* ✚ HOB *(Male)*

In spite of his conventional manner, a Hob often likes to think outside of the box. For this reason, the Weregirl may find him attractive and he'll be intrigued by her. An older Hob can be a mentor to a young Weregirl and help her with her career, and it is probable that this relationship will turn physical, as there is a natural chemistry between them. The Weregirl is not particularly impressed with material wealth, but she does find power utterly fascinating. The mature Hob may be able to put up with some of her erratic behavior in exchange for the pleasure of her company and he may even be able to help her over some of the rough times. They can form a lasting relationship, although they are less likely than some to start a family together. One such couple I know spend their free time exploring the world instead of settling down in suburbia. He's got the resources and she's got the adventurous spirit. She pushes him to take chances and he appreciates it.

WEREGIRL *(Female)* ✚ FAUN *(Male)*

Weregirls base a great deal of their interactions on their sexual appeal, so they may get frustrated with the Faun. He isn't as susceptible to her seduction techniques as other types may be, and she can get impatient with him. Fauns are somewhat naïve, but they have instincts about types who can potentially threaten their protected world, so they will usually avoid the Weregirl in the beginning.

You won't see a lot of interactions between these two forest folk. However, it is possible for her to lure him in with her softer side if she sets her mind to it. She can get validation about her sex appeal from other creatures and may not pressure him to give this to her the way another type might. They can have a pleasant if somewhat tepid relationship unless she allows her propensity for addictions to take hold or gets bored and decides to seek a new partner.

I have two friends who fit this category and bring out the best in each other. She encourages him to stand up for himself, as Fauns can be somewhat passive, and he puts her at ease with his generally placid temperament.

WEREGIRL *(Female)* **+ VAMPIRE** *(Male)*

These two have an almost instant attraction, but it is also ultimately fraught with tension. According to lore, Werewolves and Vampires are natural-born enemies, but this isn't necessarily the case and they do have similarities. They have both developed aspects of themselves to guard against feeling like outcasts. They often appreciate each other's taste in music, clothing, and art, even though it may be different. Both are edgy, sexy, and uninhibited. Neither feels threatened by the other's dark side. Their problems arise when the Weregirl seeks nurturing from the Vampire. It is very hard for her to go without this from a partner for long, but it is not something he knows how to give easily, and this can develop into a major point of contention between them. If he can't develop his nurturing side she'll probably move on. However, the Weregirl can be the perfect Vampire muse, as evidenced by Tim Burton and Winona Ryder.

WEREGIRL *(Female)* **+ WEREWOLF** *(Male)*

These two want to run off together the moment they meet. They recognize the wild look in the other's eyes and imagine tearing each other apart—in a good way. Their dating life will be exciting and full of adventures. Their sex life will be passionate yet tender. They'll never feel lonely in each other's presence.

However, both of these types could benefit from a somewhat more stable partner. If they are acting on the darker aspects of their natures at the same time, mayhem can result. They will have to try to lovingly support each other through the tough times, and if they make it to the other side (like a very sexy couple I happen to know), a happy life together awaits them. Remember, wolves mate for life!

Same-Sex Matches

I would like to be able to match up all the same-sex couples here, but that would take another whole book! However, same-sex couples can refer to the matches above, changing the gender of one or both of the types in some cases.

Two Fairies may have a similar dynamic to the Fairy and Garden Elf and two Pixies may have a somewhat similar relationship to the one described under Pixie/Woodsman. Two Hobbies are not unlike a Hob and Hobby in the way they connect. A pair of male Werewolves and a pair of male Vampires can look to the Weregirl/Werewolf and Vamp/Vampire, respectively, to get a general idea of how they match up. There are a few same-sex matches that are worth noting, as they differ so much in dynamic from hetero matches or haven't yet been explored since they involve two of the same type.

MALE SAME-SEX MATCHES

URBAN ELF (Male) **+ URBAN ELF** (Male)

This combination can last but it rarely generates a tremendous amount of passion. The cool Urbans will appreciate each other's intelligence, sophistication, taste, and contained demeanor, but it will be hard for them to open up to each other emotionally or sexually. Both do better romantically with a more contrasting type, yet they can still enjoy a long-lasting relationship, if they accept the occasional infidelity.

URBAN ELF *(Male)* + GARDEN ELF *(Male)*

The Garden Elf will mercilessly but sweetly tease the Urban, trying to coax him out of his shell. The Urban will complain but ultimately find the Garden Elf quite charming. This match can work because both these types are romantic but somewhat detached, so they'll have fun without too much heartbreak if it ends.

GARDEN ELF *(Male)* + GARDEN ELF *(Male)*

These two are likely to stay together for a long time, perhaps forever. They understand each other so well it can feel uncanny. They are best friends as well as highly compatible lovers. Their arguments may be frequent and vocal, but they always resolve them and end up having enjoyable make-up sex. Sometimes the sexuality can leave their relationship, but the tender companionship will last. They know how to make a beautiful life together and will probably have an impeccable home and well-tended garden where they entertain friends and care for assorted animals.

GARDEN ELF *(Male)* + WOODSMAN *(Male)*

Garden Elves like the masculine strength of the Woodsman and will happily pursue one. A Woodsman who is slightly unsure about his sexual orientation may enjoy the Garden Elf's take-charge attitude when it comes to relationships and can follow happily along for the ride.

GARDEN ELF *(Male)* + GIANT *(Male)*

Just as hetero Giants can devote themselves wholeheartedly to the capture and care of a Fairy, homosexual Giants may find themselves similarly focused on Garden Elves. The Giant deeply appreciates the Garden's graceful appearance, sensitive personality, and alluring edginess. The Garden Elf likes how protective and attentive the Giant can be, although he may feel smothered at times. Giants have to be as protective of and attentive to their own needs to make this relationship last.

 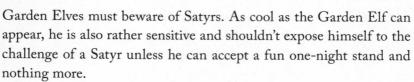

GARDEN ELF *(Male)* + SATYR *(Male)*

Garden Elves must beware of Satyrs. As cool as the Garden Elf can appear, he is also rather sensitive and shouldn't expose himself to the challenge of a Satyr unless he can accept a fun one-night stand and nothing more.

GARDEN ELF *(Male)* + HOB *(Male)*

Garden Elves love the good life, and they can depend on a generous Hob to provide them with this. The Hob can be especially vulnerable to the Garden's charms, so if he is going to enter into this relationship emotionally he must be sure the Elf has a similar investment. However, unlike some other types, Hobs are also able to emotionally detach, so they may be able to enjoy the Garden Elf's company in spite of a lack of deep connection. The Hob brings business savvy to the table and the Garden Elf brings creativity and style, so they could be quite successful in a business partnership. This may outlast their romantic relationship.

GARDEN ELF *(Male)* **+ FAUN** *(Male)*

The Garden Elf will happily encourage the Faun to embrace his sexuality. Not every type can bring this out in the Faun, but the Garden Elf is an expert. The Faun will be grateful but also somewhat anxious about this new development, as he tends to be rather repressed. If he can go with the flow he will benefit from the attention of this gifted sexual and romantic partner.

These two might not have as much success out of the bedroom. The Garden Elf's sharp tongue and the Faun's stubborn stance may clash. They'll have to work on their communication to see this through. The Faun's skills in this area aren't very developed so it will be up to the Garden Elf to keep them together if he isn't distracted by a more flexible and available partner.

WOODSMAN *(Male)* **+ WOODSMAN** *(Male)*

Because most Woodsmen are not natural aggressors, it will be difficult for these two to take the first steps to get together. They are both accustomed to being approached by other types, so they could miss the opportunity to connect. What will probably push them toward each other is their mutual desire to raise little ones. They can make devoted fathers and still find time for nurturing their relationship. They'll also both maintain lots of friendships with female creatures who may be involved in the child-rearing process.

My Woodsman friends have the kind of family life that any straight couple would envy. They are excellent parents and keep the romance alive with regular date nights and lots of communication.

WOODSMAN (Male) + MERMAN (Male)

This very masculine combination can enjoy the rugged outdoors and a playful, tough-yet-tender sexuality. Imagine a cowboy and a surfer in love and you get the idea.

GIANT (Male) + GIANT (Male)

Two Giants can build a long-lasting relationship. They will care for each other equally and enjoy a number of common interests, from collecting beautiful objects to reading esoteric literature. They may not have the most sexually intense connection, but they can make up for lack of passion with tenderness and stability, two qualities that are important to both of them.

SATYR (Male) + SATYR (Male)

What can I say? The sex will be great. The fights will be just as epic. Most gay Satyrs won't be able to resist the opportunity to try out this volatile combination at least once in their lives. It's unlikely to last past a few sexual encounters, but occasionally two mature Satyrs can make it work for a while, especially if they allow "flexibility" (read multiple partners) in their relationship.

I have a couple of burly, tattooed Satyr friends who have a very passionate, romantic relationship. On one's birthday, the other blindfolded him and took him to a tattoo parlor to get a tiger tattooed on his chest. Then they went home and had the kind of evening that they both later described with big eyes and excited sounds.

Unfortunately, they are both very stubborn and argue constantly. I'm hoping those magical moments win out for them.

SATYR *(Male)* **+** HOB *(Male)*

Hobs can usually handle the Satyr better than other types can. As keen observers of creaturekind, Hobs recognize Satyr traits right away and don't expect more of the Satyr than what he can give. Satyrs hate expectations and feel quite free around the Hob. The Satyr is actually quite savvy in his own way, and these types respect each other. They can enjoy an invigorating, if not exclusive, sexual relationship for a long time with neither of them pressuring the other to make it into something more.

HOB *(Male)* **+** HOB *(Male)*

These two can have a very nice life together—great jobs, beautiful house, nice cars, interesting friends, perhaps one neat little pet. They may not heat up the bedroom, especially after a few years together, but they are good at sublimating romantic passion into their careers, so they won't necessarily feel a sense of regret about this.

HOB *(Male)* **+** FAUN *(Male)*

Hobs and Fauns make a very good combination. The Hob's self-assertion is a good balance for the Faun's somewhat wishy-washy tendencies. The Hob will pursue the Faun and welcome him into his life. He will also usually be the aggressor sexually. The Faun may assume a pampered role in this relationship, but he can also be quite supportive of his Hob. Because both these types are sensitive at heart, they will be attuned to each other's vulnerabilities. Of course, they are also both quite stubborn and can get into battles of will, but the communicative Hob will usually know how to guide them out of these once he calms himself down.

 ### FAUN *(Male)* + FAUN *(Male)*

These two may be too alike to generate much sexual tension, but they are certain to make good companions. They'll particularly enjoy watching and playing sports together. They'll also be able to discuss movies and books and share simple, quality low-calorie meals. They may spend a long time hanging out as platonic friends if one or both of them hasn't fully accepted his attraction to other male creatures. It could be hard for them to move to the next stage of the relationship unless one asserts himself, something that doesn't come naturally to Fauns. If this happens it could pay off for both of them.

 ### VAMPIRE *(Male)* + WEREWOLF *(Male)*

These intense types can have a combative relationship, with the Vampire dominating. This is one of the most eccentric combinations, and rare, since according to lore these types, especially the male versions, are natural born enemies. If they get together, there can be a shocking amount of passion and also aggression.

FEMALE SAME-SEX MATCHES

WOOD NYMPH *(Female)* + DRYAD *(Female)*

The Wood Nymph and the Dryad can make beautiful things happen but they aren't the most sexually compatible match. Both these types like to nurture and be nurtured, but primarily in that order, and they might get a little restless with their partners attentive ways. The Wood Nymph especially seeks a challenge, even if its sometimes unconscious. These two intuitive creatures might sense that there will be problems down the line and avoid each other, in spite of an immediate physical attraction.

WOOD NYMPH *(Female)* + URBAN ELF *(Female)*

The Urban Elf's slight, feminine edge will intrigue the Wood Nymph and she will be drawn to her the way a straight Wood Nymph would be drawn to a male Urban. However, the tenderness hidden in the female Urban is more developed than in her male counterpart. The Wood Nymph will enjoy coaxing this sweetness out of her partner. These two could have a very long-lasting union.

WOOD NYMPH *(Female)* + BANSHEE *(Female)*

The tender moments will be profound, the sex will be hot, the fights will be high pitched. There is just so much estrogen in this combination that it might be hard to make it last. But afterward the poetry and songs produced may make any heartbreak worth it.

URBAN ELF *(Female)* + URBAN ELF *(Female)*

Other couples might envy the way these two Elves relate to each other. They have every interest in common and their styles are so similar that they probably share all of their clothes. Two Urban Elf females will bring out the domestic aspects of each other's personalities more than any other type can. The living environment created by two Urban Elves is welcoming and lovely, full of books and interesting objects. The food they serve and eat is nourishing and delicious, as opposed to the pastries and coffee they might consume for most meals if they lived alone. They nurture each other in equal measure and give each other a profound sense of security. Their sex life is loving, loyal, and expressive. While they may be shy or reserved with other types, they can be their warmest, most open-hearted selves when they are together.

I know a couple that fits the above description perfectly—it makes me wish I was as sexually attracted to Urban Elf females as I am to Satyrs (and that they were attracted to me).

URBAN ELF *(Female)* + HOBBY *(Female)*

These smart, witty creatures have a good chance of staying together for a long time. Each will feel that they have finally met their intellectual match, and they understand each other's underlying sensitivity. The more aggressive Hobby can help the somewhat shy Urban Elf come out of her shell, and when she does emerge she will reveal an unexpected level of sensuality that will further inspire the Hobby.

URBAN ELF *(Female)* + BROWNIE *(Female)*

This is a very workable combination. These two creatures are quite practical and smart and they'll have a lot to talk about and experience together. The Urban Elf is a bit less volatile and even though she appears serious, she'll know how to cheer up the sometimes moody Brownie better than almost any other type.

FAIRY *(Female)* + PIXIE *(Female)*

These two can really charm people with their charisma. The more extroverted Pixie will run the show, but the Fairy enjoys a certain amount of attention as well. They might not stay together long, however, once the novelty wears off. There just isn't that much tension to keep them engaged with each other.

 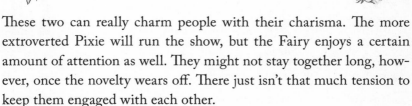

FAIRY *(Female)* + HOBBY *(Female)*

The Hobby and Fairy are as well suited to each other as the Hob and Fairy are. The Hobby takes care of business and the Fairy takes care of pleasure. They work and play well together. The Hobby makes the Fairy laugh and makes sure she is well cared for; the Fairy gives the Hobby a sense of security and pride.

The same issues that affect the male Hob and Fairy will threaten this couple. The Fairy may grow restless but feel unable to communicate it, and the Hobby may grow resentful. They'll have to work hard to stay together if this happens. Hobby Ellen DeGeneres and Fairy Anne Heche split up after about three years together.

FAIRY *(Female)* **+ BROWNIE** *(Female)*

The very femme Fairy will be attracted to the tom-creatureishly attractive Brownie and vice versa. They complement each other nicely and bring out each other's most sensual traits. The problems arise when the rather high-strung Fairy takes offense at some offhand remark made by her Brownie. Fairy anger is unexpectedly biting and can in turn cause the Brownie to react. These two can feud for long periods of time and possibly never fully forgive each other.

FAIRY *(Female)* **+ VAMP** *(Female)*

Vamps love Fairies and will be especially attracted to the light side of the Fairy personality. Fairies have their share of darkness, so they will understand the Vamp better than many types do. This can sometimes be a perfect combination for a sensitive, romantic Vamp seeking the sweet but strong love-of-her-life.

MERMAID *(Female)* **+ HOBBY** *(Female)*

Mermaids need more attention than Fairies, but they are also better at expressing their needs directly. The Hobby will be able to meet the Mermaid's needs more easily than the Fairy's, thus reducing the likelihood that the Mermaid will stray. Ellen DeGeneres and Portia de Rossi are an example of a happy Hobby/Mermaid marriage match.

MERMAID *(Female)* + BROWNIE *(Female)*

Mermaids who may not have experimented with same-sex relationships before will be most comfortable starting this exploration with the help of a Brownie. The Brownie is pretty and feminine enough to seem familiar, yet has the right amount of tom-creaturishness to provide the tension and novelty that Mermaids seek. The Brownie will probably initiate this relationship. She'll be quite worshipful of the Mermaid and, of course, Mermaids love this. The Brownie will feel special just basking in the Mermaid's presence. However, problems can arise if the Mermaid is distracted by another creature, even momentarily. The sometimes vindictive Brownie won't take well to this and may lash out before leaving for good.

TESS *(Female)* + TESS *(Female)*

The security and stability this pair offers each other is unusual. Very few types can establish such a nurturing home environment. The problem is that two Tesses don't really create enough tension for a very romantic relationship. Tesses tend to like to have someone to care for but are somewhat less comfortable receiving love. If these two can take turns giving and receiving they may be able to keep the flame alive.

BANSHEE *(Female)* + WEREGIRL *(Female)*

This is a very sexy couple. They can hardly keep their hands off each other, but the connection is deeper than that. The Banshee can help the Weregirl stay healthy, teaching her to express her feelings directly and creatively rather than acting out. The Weregirl's charms unfold magnificently in the presence of the Banshee to whom she is so attracted and who she admires so much. A certain famous actress and her presumed deejay girlfriend may be this combination.

BROWNIE *(Female)* + BROWNIE *(Female)*

This common combo has the opposite benefits and weaknesses of what Wood Nymphs and Banshees experience together. The tender moments will be less frequent, the sex will be of secondary importance, and there won't be that many hot fights. The upside: these two could stay together a long time or maybe even always.

VAMP *(Female)* + WEREGIRL *(Female)*

The Vamp, with her attraction to all things dark and dangerous, will sniff out the Weregirl's hidden pain and be wildly drawn to her. The Weregirl may in turn be attracted to the Vamp's glamorous, alluring exterior that hides a sensitive soul. This love combination is more difficult for the Vamp, who may find herself feeling betrayed by the Weregirl's restlessness. Vamps would do well to proceed with caution. One of my dear Vamp friends had her heart viciously broken by a Weregirl.

Astro-mythology

ften, though not always, types tend to be born under the same astrological signs. If yours doesn't match, check out your rising sign and moon!

ARIES
Woodsmen, Pixies

TAURUS
Fairies, Brownies, Hobs, Hobbies

GEMINI
Fauns, Werewolves, Weregirls

CANCER
Urban Elves (male and female)

LEO
Mermaids, Woodsmen, Pixies

VIRGO
Giants, Tesses, Hobs, Hobbies

LIBRA
Giants, Fairies, Garden Elves, Pixies

SCORPIO
Satyrs, Banshees, Werewolves, Weregirls, Vampires, Vamps

SAGITTARIUS
Wood Nymphs, Centaurs, Woodsmen

CAPRICORN
Brownies, Urban Elves (female), Fauns

AQUARIUS
Tree Elves, Dryads, Fauns

PISCES
Tree Elves, Dryads, Mermaids, Mermen

In addition to signs you may fall under, there are certain signs that govern the different types. This does not mean that if you are this sign, you are necessarily this type; it is just that the iconic characteristics of the sign relate to the type in some way.

ARIES, the charmingly self-involved baby of astrology, is the sign that governs Pixies and Woodsmen.

TAURUS, the bull, rules strong-minded Hobbies and Hobs.

GEMINI, the sign of the twins, governs Werewolves and Weregirls, who have two distinct personalities.

CANCER, the sensitive crab, governs male and female Urban Elves, who appear to wear a hard shell (observe their tortoise shell frames) that hides a tender soul.

LEO, the powerful lion, rules Banshees and Satyrs, although oddly most Banshees and Satyrs are not actually born under this sign.

VIRGO, the rather reserved virgin, rules the Tess and Giant types.

LIBRA, ruled in astrology by the planet Venus in all her loveliness, in turn rules the attractive and rather feminine Fairy and Garden Elf.

SCORPIO, sign of sex and death, rules the Vamp and Vampire, and they are proud of it. They may even lie and say they are born under Scorpio to make the right impression.

SAGITTARIUS, the centaur archer, rules the Centaur, for obvious reasons, as well as the creative, goal-oriented Wood Nymph.

CAPRICORN, the goat sign, rules the Brownie and deceptively strong and stubborn Faun.

AQUARIUS, the water beaver, oversees freethinking Dryads and Tree Elves.

PISCES, the fish, rules the Mermaid and Merman, although most Mermaids are not water signs but more aggressive fire signs.

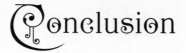Conclusion

So where does all this leave me—a single Wood Nymph still lost and alone in the forest?

I'm relying a lot on my female friends these days—a flock of Fairies, a small band of Banshees, assorted Urban Elves, Tesses, Vamps, and Dryads. We meet monthly in my living room and write poetry to help us forget about our creature troubles. As a Wood Nymph, I have to keep writing. It's what will get me through even if the perfect Centaur or Woodsman doesn't show up. Maybe some of my Wood Nymph tendencies will continue to soften. Maybe I'll finally find some peace and satisfaction just being alone with my baby Merwood (a mermaid/wood nymph in training) and her brother (whose type hasn't emerged yet), my friends, and my work. The journey into the dark dating wood is scary sometimes, but ultimately we'll all see the light glimmering through the leaves, dappling our faces with shadow and shine as we emerge, coupled or peacefully alone, with a little more knowledge of others and, most important, ourselves.

Acknowledgments

If Lydia Wills had not realized the potential of this book, it might never have been written. She is a constant source of support and inspiration. According to Lydia, Reg E. Cathey got her "fired up" about this project. Lydia also discovered the genius artist Fumi Mini Nakamura, who brought the words to life with her illustrations. Benjamin Adams and Rachel Mannheimer at Bloomsbury made it all happen and I am grateful for their sensitive editing skills.

Many of my friends helped guide and inspire this book or just supported me emotionally during the sometimes grueling "research" process. They include Paul Monroe, Sera Gamble, Carmen Staton, Tracey Porter, Suzy Sanchez, Sarah Hechtman, Sara Turbeville, Caron Post, Reina Escobar, Rachel Resnick, Marjo Maisterra, Sandra Bossier, Morningstar and Michael, Steve Erickson and Lori Precious, Yxta Maya Murray, and Molly Bendall. A special thank you to Carol Blake and Dr. Hari Bhajan Khalsa for helping me learn how to manage my Wood Nymph nature.

All of my students enrich my life and my work. The very talented members of my critique group have been especially wonderful. They are Jennifer Sky Band, Rocio Carlos-Gonzales, Liz Dubelman, Jeni McKenna, and Margo Valentine.

I would like to thank my editors on other projects for keeping me writing, and therefore not only employed but sane. They are Tara Weikum at Harper, Giovanni Arduino at Elliot Edizioni, and Jennifer

Joseph at Manic D. Jason Yarn and Alyssa Reuben at Paradigm always make sure things run smoothly.

Wood Nymphs only like to be photographed by people they trust. Nicolas Sage took the author photo, with the assistance of Robert Kozek. Mandy O'Hanlon's help with my hair and makeup made me feel especially at ease.

Finally, thanks to my brother, Gregg Marx, my mother, Gilda Block, and my two children, Jasmine Angelina Schuette and Sam Alexander Schuette. I love you.

A Note on the Author

FRANCESCA LIA BLOCK is a bestselling author of many works of fiction, nonfiction, and poetry—from the groundbreaking Weetzie Bat young adult series to a collection of magic-realist erotica. Her numerous awards include the Margaret A. Edwards Award for lifetime achievement in young adult literature, and her work has been published around the world. Born in Los Angeles, she lives there still with her two children.